Colette and the Incest Taboo

Colette and the Incest Taboo

That Most Disturbing of Drives

Carol Mastrangelo Bové

ANTHEM PRESS

Anthem Press
An imprint of Wimbledon Publishing Company
www.anthempress.com

This edition first published in UK and USA 2025
by ANTHEM PRESS
75–76 Blackfriars Road, London SE1 8HA, UK
or PO Box 9779, London SW19 7ZG, UK
and
244 Madison Ave #116, New York, NY 10016, USA

British Library Cataloguing-in-Publication Data
A catalogue record for this book is available from the British Library.

Library of Congress Cataloging-in-Publication Data
A catalog record for this book has been requested.
2024940648

ISBN-13: 978-1-83999-048-9 (Hbk)
ISBN-10: 1-83999-048-1 (Hbk)

Cover Credit: © Henri Manuel / Roger-Viollet

This title is also available as an e-book.

For Pauline Rose Moritz
Sister and Friend

CONTENTS

ACKNOWLEDGMENTS

I would like to thank Daniel T. O'Hara and Jeffrey R. DiLeo for enabling me to spend time with the incredible Colette. Julia Kristeva, too, with her book on the female genius, made it possible for me to undertake this study. She brought me back to a writer whose talents I had not previously recognized.

Paul A. Bové as ever helped me a great deal, though psychoanalytic writing is not his preferred mode. My daughter Laura, her husband José, and their child, my grandson, José Paul, provided support via meals and games to refresh and remind me that there is more to life than literary criticism.

Finally, I want to thank Sue Super for her beautiful drawing of the old lion, which conveys so well the animality of Colette's prose. Her work also reawakens in me memories of our time together many years ago at Notre Dame Academy, Rittenhouse Sq., Philadelphia.

Photo of Colette

Introduction

THAT MOST MAJESTIC AND DISTURBING OF DRIVES: COLETTE'S WORK AND LIFE

This book examines what is the fundamental social prohibition, the incest taboo hovering over Colette's writing. I am using the term "incest" to refer to sexual relations and/or desires between not only biological parents and children (incestuous) but also between individuals who function as parent and child in their principal interactions (incestual). Her fiction shows how women's relationships often emerge from incestuous or incestual longings and reproduce parent–child experiences. She explores how to cope with the serious problems that develop as they confront the social norms inhibiting such relations and blocking their aspirations.

The incest taboo is a contradictory concept in that it enables the existence of society while at the same time prohibiting certain forms of social behavior. The research on the topic is complex and often focuses on how the prohibition, which exists virtually everywhere and at all times, came about. Scholars consider the degree to which it is based in human biology, citing the fact that animals do not often mate with their relatives. They have also done research on the cultural roots of the taboo, using evidence from many times and places to show that "the prohibition was not simply negative: it forced men to marry outside of their clan and thus to forge social relations with the outside." Claude Lévi-Strauss in his *The Elementary Structures of Kinship* is the prominent proponent of this theory.[1]

While Colette does not as far as I know discuss the emergence of the taboo, this study of the prohibition in her work and films dealing with it leads to a fuller understanding of the prohibition and the question of how it arose. Sigmund Freud's elaboration of the myth in *Totem and Taboo* that "primordial sons killed their father in order to possess their mother," suffered terrible guilt as a result and thus instituted the prohibition is by no means documented truth.[2] The myth does, however, reveal the psychological roots of the taboo to the degree that the story focuses on guilt, as do Colette's novels. Thus, this examination of her writing as well as the films dealing with it helps to understand the prohibition and its emergence including the way incest changes and deepens because of her work.

Given the rich variety of Colette's writing and biography, as well the films dealing with them, many other texts are relevant to my topic, for example, her novels *Break of Day* (1928) and *The Pure and the Impure* (1932) as well as Jacqueline Audrey's movie adaptation of *Gigi* (1949), and Stephen Frears film version of *Chéri* (2009). For this book in the Anthem symplokē Studies in Theory, I have selected her best-loved texts representative of a central component of Colette's thought and read them to some extent through the lens of Kristeva's theory to help understand the taboo. The protagonists in these narratives are women on the verge. That is to say, they are dealing with incestuous longing in ways that point to but leave unclear the outcome of their struggles, as the following chapters show in greater detail in my focus on Colette's thinking on female psychology.

My examination of the novelist reveals the incestuous desire many earlier readers fail to see when focusing on the surface of the texts. This includes the focus on how her autobiographical novel, *La Maison de Claudine*, idealizes the past. They neglect this topic in *Chéri* and *Gigi* as well, in both of which she reinvents the trope of a courtesan who falls in love. Some recent theories and practice support surface reading but my approach is different.[3] Inspired by Julia Kristeva's work, exceptional in the body of criticism on Colette, this book takes seriously the pressures of incest and its taboo in her novels and supplies a new understanding of the incestuous desire at their core via a close reading.

My approach opens an interpretation of literary history unavailable until now: her novels give a compelling voice to the conflicted psychology of women and reveal her contributions to modernist literature. I show how this voice expands our notion of modern art and, in fact, expands the idea of modernism itself. It is likely that Colette chooses the names of her characters, Marcel D'Avricourt, the gay actor in *La Maison de Claudine*, and Gilberte, Gigi's full name, because of their associations with her contemporary, Proust, the modernist novelist of sexual codes par excellence in France at the time. Although the comparison between the two writers is not the principal topic of my study, I do discuss some of the similarities and differences between the two as modernist novelists. While the movement often portrays an unconventional woman, it is significant that Colette's protagonists are exceptional in their struggle with the incest taboo.

My earlier work on modernist literature focused on Julia Kristeva's contributions to psychoanalytic criticism and theory as well as to the study of this novelist.[4] Arguably the most significant psychoanalytic author alive today and a major critic of Colette, she connects her writing to an increasingly open language of sexuality underlying customs, law, and human freedoms. The psychoanalytic critic was for me the impetus to discover the novelist I had misconstrued in my youth as a writer dealing primarily with a close relationship with her cats and dogs. The thought-provoking third volume of Kristeva's trilogy, *Female Genius: Colette*,[5] led me to explore the interplay between women's psychology and the limits they face, with special emphasis on the incest taboo. This is the path that engaged me in the close readings of the three novels I include in this volume along with Vincente Minnelli's adaptation of *Gigi* and Wash Westmoreland's bio picture, *Colette*. My goal is to understand better Colette's work in the context of literary modernism and women's internal struggles as they seek greater autonomy in a world that, while progressing socially, continues to challenge this marginalized group.

Kristeva writes on Colette's incestuous and bisexual voices and recent developments in psychoanalysis in an essay previously unpublished in English. I have included my translation of it, "Neither Depression nor Perversion: Colette in Bloom,"[6] in this book to discuss it in the chapters that follow. For her, Colette's novels have an ethical dimension to the degree that she forges a new tongue enabling human beings to progress beyond incestuous desire and bisexuality as pathologies. Instead, they are human characteristics often connected to creativity.[7]

Colette and Kristeva engage in questions of gender and power in ways that are quite different from those we often see in the United States. Their thinking on identity politics is complex and unlike that of American multiculturalists who reject their critique of aspects of feminism. Considered both feminist and nonfeminist, they are perfect examples to examine in the debate over the influence of American models in France.[8]

Furthermore, Kristeva's oeuvre supplies the theoretical context, which enables a fuller appreciation of these novels, as well as of the contributions of Minnelli's and Westmoreland's films to Colette's studies, as I show. The French Bulgarian's thought, particularly on the maternal and abjection, for example, in *Female Genius: Colette* (2002), "Stabat Mater" (1987), and *Powers of Horror* (1982), contributes to an understanding of the psychology of women and social transformation today.[9] Her psychoanalytic model locates the sources of human behavior in the psyche. It offers the potential to understand, confront, and in this way cope better with impulses both pleasurable and dangerous to individual and social well-being. In other words, her theory examines women's need to understand the stranger within themselves and to come to terms with the psychic and interpersonal conflicts, which social norms and inadequate mental health care—she is a practicing psychoanalyst—make difficult to confront. In brief, for Kristeva, Colette's novels engage the reader in an examination of abjection, the ambiguities connected to the parent–child relation, and the possibility of a perspective of care or generosity toward both self and other.

From a Kristevan perspective, in her female characters, she creates a psychic formation, especially incestuous desire, which is not a "perversion" but rather a creative and healthy confrontation with and subversion of the status quo. This is not to say that Colette condones incest but rather that the novel enables the reader to reflect on incestuous longings and better cope with them while enjoying the beauty of her writing. Briefly said, her fiction offers knowledge, therapy, and aesthetic pleasure in ways previously unrecognized.

I focus on three of her best-known, most admired novels and their translation in examining the underpinnings of her prose. These include *Chéri* (1920), *La Maison de Claudine* (*My Mother's House*) (1922), and *Gigi* (1944), along with two movies, one adapting her work, Vincente Minnelli's *Gigi* (1958), and the other depicting her life, Wash Westmoreland's *Colette* (2018).[10] This body of work illustrates well the significance of the problem of incest in her writing and films dealing with it.

Women's longstanding battle to free themselves of abusive relationships, which patriarchal France of the early twentieth century made particularly difficult and dangerously attractive, as these texts show, still is an arduously complicated task. Colette's work on this front is timely given the examples of individuals who abuse their power over others and themselves in the guise of playing a parental role. These include for example, couples in which partners exercise excessive control, athletic coaches and priests who become predators of young people, and those who force individuals in the LGBTQ community to struggle to live their gender identity as if they were not adults. Thus, the focus on parent–child relationships in Colette contributes not only to modernist literature but also to the understanding of current problems women meet with in developing control over their lives and the emotional well-being that goes with it.

Beyond her literary criticism and theory, Kristeva, as a practicing psychoanalyst, recognizes the presence of the harmful effects of treating a love object as a child. In the following quotation from her book on the novelist, she begins by making clear that she is speaking of incestuous fantasy and the psychological ramifications resulting from treating a partner as if she or he were a child, as Westmoreland will depict Willy's treatment of Colette in his film. She says:

> Not to be confused with the *reality* of incest and the psychic wounds it inflicts on the children who are its victims, the *unconscious incestuous fantasy* participates in our essentially perverse sexuality, which can even

> determine the choice of partners and fix them in archaic relationships of the parent–child type (*incestual*, in other words), which exert an influence over the couple that is as jubilant as it is risky and inexorable.[11]

Her comment acknowledges the complexity of such relationships, suggesting the joy but more so the increasing danger and difficulty Colette encounters in her engagement with Willy and in the attempts to extricate herself from him. Other research in psychology recognizes the widespread, enduring problem of such relations. Paul-Claude Racamier defined the incestual concept in his *L'Inceste et l'incestuel* in 1995.[12] Cognitive behavioral psychology, more common in the United States than psychoanalysis, also recognizes the problem. Robert Epstein, for example, examines this issue in a recent broad study of the harmful effects of treating a love object as a child.[13]

The clearest example of the problem of incest in Colette's life is her relationship at the age of forty-four with her sixteen-year-old stepson Bertrand de Jouvenel in 1920. He is the son of her second husband Henry de Jouvenel from an earlier marriage. This rapport develops after she wrote *Chéri*, in which she depicts a similar liaison, but not with a family member. I am, however, primarily interested in her writing: the Colette who appears in these novels with reference to the real-life woman who created them. I am discussing what we can call the unconscious in Colette's writing as its work appears in her language. In other words, I am writing a critical psychoanalytic book, the nature of which cannot and need not rely mostly on the positive facts offered by the biographical narrative. My Colette is not primarily the person who walked the earth, but the authority at work in the texts, the "Colette" created, working, and stimulating response in writing.

In my reading, she is most interested in love as a complex experience fraught with unequal power relations and including sexual drive in its encounter with the taboos of incest and, in *La Maison de Claudine*, bisexuality. She has written: "Why should I stop my hand from gliding over this paper to which for so many years I've confided what I know about myself, what I've tried to hide, what I've invented and what I've guessed? At no time has the catastrophe of love, in all its phases and consequences, formed a part of the true intimate life of a woman" (*Break of Day*).[14]

Chéri focuses on the passion between the aging courtesan in her fifties, Léa, and twenty-five-year-old Fred, better known under his eponymous nickname. The novel appears at times to celebrate incestual desire and to that extent victory over patriarchal norms. The plot also retells the story of a high-class prostitute who falls in love for the first time. Examples include Alexandre Dumas fils's *La Dame aux Camélias*, Giuseppe Verdi's *La Traviata*, based on Dumas's play and novel, and Colette's echoing of this trope in *Gigi*, examined here in Chapter 3.

Patriarchal society works as a destructive force in the background of this narrative, for instance, in Léa's life as a courtesan, despite its financial rewards. A harmful element also appears in Chéri's silence, particularly concerning his emotions. He displays the masculine tendency often valued under patriarchy to be impassive.

At the same time, the patriarchal prohibition of incest motivates Léa's break with Chéri and is positive. Incestuous desires are destructive in part because they bring about debilitating guilt, for example, over the effect on Chéri's appealing wife, Edmée. They also lead to a stunting of growth in "the child." It is a prohibition that also has a biological as well as social part, relevant to Léa's aging, beyond the genetic predisposition to disease in blood relatives, which is not an issue here.

Chéri is much more than the plot first appears, offering fascinating, nuanced protagonists including the unconscious emotions and thoughts of both "mother" and "child." Furthermore, the novel raises questions with significance for us in 2024 such as: how best to live with love when it conflicts with social and biological realities and is vulnerable to debilitating anxiety and/or abusive behavior?

It is testimony to Colette's ability as a novelist that she can convey the perspectives of both "mother" and "child" while creating a coherent prose revealing unconscious desire and multiple identities. The protagonists and the limited third-person narrator articulate indirectly the underlying nuances of Chéri's silences and his relationship with his "good mother." Léa collapses on the one-month anniversary of Chéri's marriage to Edmée, simply crying out "Chéri"![15] The courtesan notices with distress, unable to understand adequately her conflicted feelings on her aging, the marriage, the young couple's lovemaking in Italy, and the mark he has left on the carved wood during a past angry encounter in their rose-colored bedroom. The narrator describes her state soon after as an "animal spasm" while Léa speculates with bittersweet humor and irony on a poetic turn in her thoughts as she contemplates "the beautiful hand, which left its trace and is now turning away from her for good."[16]

Here, both Chéri and Léa behave in inexplicable ways—he is silent, she simply cries out his name, then, in contrast to her distress, assumes a detached, humorous, and ironic air in commenting on his hand. In this context, Léa, the principal protagonist, is struggling with desire for the young man, sensing its inappropriate nature. The analysis of significant passages like these reveals unconscious desire in Colette's language in the portrayal of both Léa and Chéri, as the next chapter in the novel shows in greater detail.

An element of their love emphasizes the importance of physical beauty as something that arouses desire in and confers nobility on human beings. Her blue eyes and his thick eyelashes, for example, play a vital role in their falling and staying in love, as the opening of the novel makes clear. Their physical characteristics mark them as aesthetically significant—they are both beautiful to behold, a fact that is a precious, universal value for Colette in her writing and one that can be dangerous in its consequences as in this narrative.

What dominates beyond their physical attraction and attractiveness, understood in both the conventional sense and in that they are exceptionally beautiful bodies worthy of aesthetic appreciation, is their mother/child relationship. Léa has played the role of "good mother" for over a period of six years, in contrast with his biological mother, Madame Peloux, who is guilty of serious neglect. The "bad mother" has resulted in weaknesses in Chéri's physical and mental development, though his beauty and charm continue to dominate.

Another key part of their relationship is the gap between them, beyond the age difference, which derives at least in part from the universal human difficulty of understanding one another completely. According to Léa, as she explains in problematic terms, Chéri "speaks another language," that of "a Chinese or a Negro," and often does not directly communicate his thoughts or emotions to her. Colette makes clear that he, and at times, Léa herself, are not able to do so.[17]

The conclusion of the novel raises more questions than it answers about the relationship: how are these two individuals to live well given their passion for each other? Both separating and staying together are unworkable. The social reality is that to continue their life together will bring increasing guilt to the lovers. The biological truth is that Léa's aging will make their attraction to each other problematic given the values assigned to a beautiful, youthful body, especially by these two individuals. Separation is the result, bringing intense pain to each for what is likely to be the rest of their lives, with Chéri committing suicide at an early age in the sequel to the novel, *La Fin de Chéri*.

Thus, the text implies that Léa and Chéri's relationship cannot continue unchecked if one is to live and mature. In *Chéri*, incestual desires lead, because of the natural aging/biological process, to an old age/death in "the parent," which results not only in decreasing attraction between the two but also in "the child" feeling lonely and abandoned. The novel ends with these consequences visible in both protagonists. Furthermore, Colette has Chéri put an end to his life without Léa in the later volume.

La Maison de Claudine (1922), completed after a visit back to her birthplace with her stepson Bertrand in 1921, complicates the narrative of love in its encounter with social norms and biological realities by introducing the themes of bisexuality and same-gender attraction. The taboos against both same-sex desire and incest surface primarily in the narrator's relationship with her mother, Sido, and in the chapter "Paris Fashions." Critics as renowned as Doris Lessing read the autobiographical novel as an idyllic recreation of Colette's childhood.

An idealized view of her early years sometimes appears, along with insight into the precious imagination and resistance to social norms of children, especially the author herself and her child, Bel Gazou. A closer reading of the novel uncovers the narrator's unconscious desire for her mother, often the source of the idealization, and the guilt that results. Chapter 2 examines in more detail the inadequate translations of the novel, which help to account for the misreading of it.

My new, forthcoming translation reveals the reading of the novel presented here. This interpretation grows out of my engagement in the debates on translation studies, a discipline that has emerged in recent years, as well as on psychoanalytic theory and criticism. While literary translation had often considered the rendering of a creative writer's work a transparent process, my sense of it, developed over years of translating literary criticism, and now fiction, confirms what others in the emerging field understand.[18] Literary translation, like all complex writing, derives at least in part from the translator's culture, formation, and research. Balancing a careful close reading of the original with a rendering that is proper to an English-speaking audience in 2024, I have made choices based on the French, on the target audience, and also on my formation and research as a psychoanalytic reader of world literature.

My effort in this new translation is to recreate the spirit of the original French, particularly its long-overlooked implicit themes of incest and bisexuality. The translation makes clearer than earlier English versions that the voicing of heterosexual norms filters that of the bisexual narrator and author and their incestuous desires. The new translation sees the text primarily as the conflicted voice of a bisexual woman coping with the incest taboo rather than as idealized memories.

La Maison de Claudine, one of the most complex of Colette's novels, raises the question of how to confront such taboos. How does one live the conflicting responses to the social order, that is, the alternating emotions of abjection and celebratory victory over such distress? Here Colette portrays a subject who suffers greatly not only because of oppressive patriarchal norms but also as a result of a masochistic tendency within herself that appears to submit to such limits, as I explained in my earlier reading of this challenging text.[19] On one level, the novel stages an at times self-destructive narrator who has broken with her mother, represented in the opening expression of guilt: her feelings of regret and unworthiness. The ending of the volume on her own child, Bel Gazou, who will grow out of the sensual, imaginative being she once was, understood in the context of the preceding chapters, reprises the break with the mother. At a deeper level, however, Colette at times celebrates victory over oppression from within and without, though tinged with dread. In other words, there occurs an identification and union with a female figure who incorporates incestuous and bisexual desires, a source of both pleasure and pain.

Opening chapters of the novel allude to the first-person narrator's feelings of regret, suggesting not only that she has turned from her mother in moving to Paris and leading a different life but also, in the context of the chapters that follow, that she worries and suffers unconscious anxiety. One recalls that Colette herself is engaged in an incestuous relationship with her stepson, Bertrand, while writing this. Here, the narrator is unable to speak of incestuous and gay desire. She writes that her mother's death and the loss of the magical world she created is one "of which I have ceased to be worthy." On the same page, the narrator implies that despite her detailed descriptions of house and garden, her words are inadequate, "Is it worth while, I wonder, seeking for adequate words to describe the rest?"[20]

Strategically inserted between the opening chapter and the one entitled "Jealousy" comes "The Savage" and its critique of heterosexual love in the description of Sido's first husband's abominable behavior in buying his young wife. Via this insertion, the critique of heterosexual love serves to add value to and emphasize the theme of same-sex desire, which is present in "Jealousy" when read in the context of the rest of the volume.

This chapter reveals her intense love for Sido, which goes beyond affection for a mother. Embedded in the episode on the eponymous jealousy experienced by Colette the father, lies that felt by Colette the daughter/narrator. Romantic and sexual allusions including blushing, breasts, and coquetry make clear her desire for Sido. One clue is her astonishment at how intensely pleased she is upon hearing her mother's elegant footstep, seeing her approach as she turns the corner, followed by resentment when her mother inquires after her father instead of her. Ironically, the narrator draws attention to her lack of consciousness, that is, her inability to articulate her desire directly and her own illicit longings, by pointing out "the ferocity of love," to which she was blind at fifteen, but which she now believes she understands. In this way, Colette qualifies her more usual critique of heterosexual love by depicting her parents' devotion to each other.

The next chapter, "The Little One," reveals that what is essential to her sense of who she is lies in the intelligent mother, illuminated, for example, with her thimble in the window of their home as the young daughter returns. Colette makes clear that the young narrator is returning both to her house and to her identity as her mother's daughter after the Thursday break from school enjoyed with her rambunctious, conventional, and at times foolish friends.

Chapters from the middle and end of the book, "Paris Fashions" and "The Seamstress," reveal emotions and behaviors associated with incestuous and bisexual desires, respectively: fear, pleasure, breaking the norm, silence, and guilt. Colette links mother and daughter (including the narrator's own daughter), along with the gay actor, Marcel d'Avricourt, from the chapter "Paris Fashions" via their voice and sewing and in this way conveys illicit desire. The first-person narrator subtly reveals both the mother's and the child's perspectives, for instance in the final chapters of the novel in which the reader perceives the daughter's point of view: "she is too near the truth, and too natural not to know as a birthright, that all nature hesitates before that most majestic and most disturbing of instincts, and that it is wise to tremble, to be silent and to lie when one draws near to it."[21]

In this passage, Colette is unusually explicit in referring to sexual desire, including the unconscious, as "l'instinct le plus majestueux et le plus trouble."[22] I translate "l'instinct" as "drive" rather than "instinct," adopting Jean Laplanche and Jean-Bertrand Pontalis's precise psychoanalytic term. They discuss the greater precision of "pulsion" and "drive" in their discussion of the respective French and English translations of Freud's German "trieb" in their entry on "instinct/drive" in *The Language of Psycho-analysis.*[23] The effort to translate Colette more adequately into English leads to my unexpected discovery that, in the novel's context, she herself has chosen the less appropriate word, at least with the hindsight provided by Laplanche and Pontalis. She may have made this choice because it is a term more commonly used, especially in 1922 ("l'instinct" ("instinct") instead of "pulsion" ("drive")), to convey "that most majestic and disturbing of drives." I will return to her sense that the drive is majestic as well as disturbing.

Colette's foci on both a parent's and a child's perspective continue in *Gigi.* This novel goes beyond the simplistic, fairy tale-like celebration of a woman finding love with a man as a first reading might suggest. It is true, however, that it is a rosier narrative, at least on the surface, than *Chéri*, *La Maison de Claudine*, or Dumas's version of the courtesan world on which Verdi bases his opera. With a plot like that of *La Dame aux Camélias* and *La Traviata* but eliminating the heroine's death and adding the significant age difference to the lovers as she did in *Chéri*, Colette examines the presence of the paternal figure in a young girl's developing love.

Given the author's critique of heterosexual love elsewhere, the portrayal of the relationship between Gigi and Gaston Lachaille takes on special meaning.

Simone de Beauvoir recognized Colette's *La Maison de Claudine* as a significant rethinking of patriarchy, heterosexuality, and traditional forms of marriage in the chapter on "The Married Woman" in *The Second Sex* in 1949.[24]

In *Gigi*, her portrayal of the couple reflects the refinement of Colette's thinking, contemplated and experienced over years in the author's various sexual relationships with several men and women, including three marriages. This text is among the last of her novels, published in 1944. The reading of *Gigi* along with that of the two earlier novels makes clear the complexity of Colette's perspective on women's psychology in contrast to earlier literary criticism, which focuses more exclusively on the author's negative views of heterosexuality and marriage.

The incest taboo hovers over the narrative, making readers uncomfortable and engaging them in understanding the story as a whole. Gigi and Gaston's relationship is incestual in its context for two reasons. The young girl of sixteen has been interacting with a father figure twice her age with unusually intense and increasing pleasure in both. As her grandmother, Madame Alvarez puts it, "For years you [Gaston] have been giving her sweets and playthings. She [Gigi] swears by Tonton [Gaston] and by him alone".[25] There is also a reference to the affair of Gigi's grandmother, Madame Alvarez, with Gaston's father. If Gaston is in fact the grandmother's son, he would be Gigi's uncle. Furthermore, she calls him "Tonton Gaston," a colloquial term for "Uncle Gaston."

Gaston is quite the womanizer, though an unhappy one, and we learn that he has left his most recent courtesan, who tries to commit suicide, or at least she gives the impression of doing so. Madame Alvarez, the principal maternal figure in the novel, since Andrée, Gigi's biological mother, is often at the theatre where she works as a singer, cautions her granddaughter against getting to know her friends and particularly the fathers who pick them up after school In addition, Andrée expresses misgivings about Gaston, suggesting that he is not really committed to supporting the family. Thus, without directly pointing to the taboo of incest, Colette implies that not only may there be a close genetic tie between the lovers, but also added dangers threatening Gigi in her liaison with Gaston, the parental figure much older and more powerful socially than she. Gigi herself explicitly refers to his "love them and leave them" behavior with women in the past. In explaining her refusal to him, she is very aware of her possible fate in marrying him, "When you throw me over once and for all, as you did Gentiane des Cevennes when you'd had enough of her—"[26]

Thus, once again, Colette has the reader consider both the "child's" and the "parent's" perspectives: is Gigi right to pursue her passion for Gaston despite her fear that he may abuse her in the future by leaving? Is Gaston trustworthy in his relations with his young "niece" whom he claims to love? The narrative's tone, as an analysis of significant passages uncovers (see Chapter 3), warns the reader to acknowledge the dangers and bouts of anxiety accompanying the choice to follow one's desire.

Kristeva's inclusion of the importance of the individual's integration in society in her theory is particularly helpful in my examination of the ways in which Colette's writing constitutes a vehicle for her to integrate her existence in being in the world. Her book on Colette states early on in naming the originality of her work, "How to define it? As an intersection between the flesh of a woman and the world's flesh. Colette interrupts her narrative with reveries, states of mind, ordinary or extreme bodily sensations [...]. how could one name differently what she formulated with a precision so definitive that changing a single syllable would destroy the palpitating flesh of the world?"[27] These statements come closest to clarifying what Kristeva means by her enigmatic formulation of Colette's writing constituting "existence in the flesh of the world": recreating the body and mind's experience in living viscerally in their environment. She states, referring to *The Pure and the Impure*, that Colette implies that "perversion necessarily, inevitably, leads to the infantile, the memory of which (the archaic face) was situated in mother–child incest and whose purity (the sublime face) led finally to an immersion in Being. That was the only means to bathe her writing in the world's flesh."[28] As Kristeva makes clear, Colette's recreation of physical and psychic experience appears out of incestuous desire, grounded in presence, temporal unity, and I would add, memory.

Kristeva also writes:

> Neither metaphysical nor sociopolitical, the way of *being in the world* specific to Colette, which culminates in the writing *of* and *in* the world's flesh, implies a consideration of the impasses as well as the fertility of the love relationship, with its homo- and heterosexual valences. It attests to a *profound modification* of *the conception of the couple*, which feminists have not been wrong to see as a courageous beginning of women's freedom [...]. There is nothing but a constant concern for the emancipation of the subject, with a priority given to the woman subject who wishes to achieve her sensual freedom in order to maintain her curiosity and creativity in a plurality of relationships.[29]

The three novels I analyze in this book reveal Colette's understanding of how incestuous/incestual desire underlies the couple as a complex relationship encompassing 1) the older woman and younger man (*Chéri*), 2) the mother and daughter (*La Maison de Claudine*), and 3) the younger woman and the older man (*Gigi*).

While Kristeva's book emphasizing Colette's writing as an affirmation of "Existence in the flesh of the world" does not mention Heidegger, I understand this formulation of the novelist's integration in Being in connection with his work. Her fiction displays a capacity for connecting one's existence as an individual in the moment to that of others, even to the rest of the world, including its flora and fauna. She writes in a way that makes these connections across both space and time, which resembles Heidegger's ideas of "taking-as" and "care." Furthermore, her fiction explores abjection, which is related to Heidegger's notion of dread, as my concluding chapter analyzes at greater length in considering the similarities in thinking between the German philosopher and the French novelist.

According to what may be Kristeva's clearest and fullest discussion of the topics of the maternal and abjection in the first section of *Powers of Horror*, the fact that human experience normally starts with being part of a woman's body, at least in most cases, has an enduring impact on both physical and mental development. Briefly said, abjection is a complex experience deriving from the newborn's feelings of both attachment and repulsion for the mother's body. The attempt to recreate the original pleasurable attachment to the mother goes with the development of the other as authority figure. These two processes of maturation engage the human being in the acquisition of language, understood as a voicing of desire as well as a rational form of communication. For Kristeva, these developments are fraught with difficulty and may at times lead to periods of such severe depression that one is unable to speak. It is this state that she identifies as abjection, with a precision that distinguishes it from a more general condition of severe depression. In explaining how abjection arises out of a process beginning in a woman's body, Kristeva links it to Judeo-Christian thinking on the woman as a source of impurity and sin.

Before Kristeva's book on the novelist appeared, Jerry Aline Flieger's *Colette and the Fantom Subject of Autobiography* (1992) had identified the centrality of the relationship between mother and daughter in Colette's writing from a psychoanalytic perspective.[30] Without discussing incest in her book taken as a whole, she had written in her analysis of *My Mother's House*, "Sido plays the role of Gertrude, the maternal object of Hamlet's incestuous desire, the pre-Oedipal paradise from which her child has been exiled." Flieger had also traced the importance in psychoanalytic theory of the pre-Oedipal phase and the complex function of the maternal figure in it as both object of desire and lawgiver.

Furthermore, according to *Colette and the Fantom Subject of Autobiography*, Colette believes all, male and female, are bisexual.[31] Without mentioning Flieger, Kristeva says that the novelist is convinced that all women are bisexual, based especially on her comments in *Le Pur et l'impur.*[32] Thus, with at times remarkable parallels to Freud's groundbreaking work, Colette in fact talks about bisexuality in women twenty-three years before Freud's *Female Sexuality* (1931) does. He describes a woman's psyche as more often bisexual than a man's though he recognizes bisexual dispositions in everyone.[33]

While Flieger's contribution to the study of Colette is clear, her conclusion that *The Break of Day* (1928) is the better novel to the degree that it expresses less self-incrimination, melancholy, and anger than *My Mother's House* is not convincing.[34] These qualities are, I argue, precisely what make her fiction compelling, particularly in *Chéri, La Maison de Claudine*, and *Gigi*. They derive, I show, from the presence of the incest taboo and a sense of both the jouissance and fear which permeate Colette's writing. In other words, the protagonists' engagement with the prohibition brings with it both great pleasure and terrible fear. It is in this sense that the narrator of *La Maison de Claudine* speaks of "that most majestic and disturbing of drives," as mentioned above.

While shaped by Kristeva's and Flieger's theories and examination of Colette, my close reading of the three novels as well as the films dealing with her work and life open a new Colette for an understanding of modernism. *Colette and the Fantom Subject of Autobiography* does a careful reading of the novels' form in ways that reveal its modernist elements.[35] Flieger notes in particular Colette's non-straight protagonists (Chéri); circular structures, especially images of luminous circularity; cadenced, that is, rhythmic recurrences of departures and returns in *Chéri*; and the feminine textile crafts.

Thus, Colette's staging of the female encounter with the incest taboo via the unconscious in her fiction obliges literary historians to recognize her contributions to the modernist movement. The subtext of incestuous desire and the way the author expresses it in the details of both her own language and that of a translator have gone unrecognized. They endow the narratives with a fundamental unity and break ground, especially with *Chéri* and *La Maison de Claudine* in 1920–1923, given their unorthodox message and early experiment in literary modernism. Time shifts, puns, and dreams combine with the unconventional, psychologically complex, non-straight protagonist, which the reader has come to associate with the best modernist novelists, for example, Virginia Woolf and Marcel Proust. Recognizing her contribution to modernism, this book shows how Colette creates women courageously coping with the abjection and dread connected to prohibitions against incest and bisexuality.

Notes

1 Claude Lévi-Strauss, *The Elementary Structures of Kinship*, trans. James Harle Bell, John Richard von Sturmer and Rodney Needham (Boston: Beacon Press, 1969).

2 On the voluminous research on this topic, see, for example, Camille Robcis, "Lévi-Strauss's Structuralist Social Contract," *Yale French Studies*, 123 (2013): 145–165. https://www.jstor.org/stable/23645880; Carl Degler, "The Case of the Origin of the Incest Taboo," in *Search of Human Nature: The Decline and Revival of Darwinism in American Social Thought* (London: Oxford University Press, 1992), pp. 245–269. https://ebookcentral.proquest.com/lib/pitt-ebooks/reader.action?docID=3051870&ppg=258 (quoted phrases on Lévi-Strauss and Freud are from Robcis and Degler, respectively); Seymour Parker, "The Precultural Basis of the Incest Taboo: Toward a Biosocial Theory," *American Anthropologist*, vol. 78, no. 2 (June, 1976): 285–305. https://www.jstor.org/stable/675233.

3 See Stephen Best and Sharon Marcus, "Surface Reading: An Introduction," *Representations*, vol. 108, no. 1 (2009): 1–21. https://doi.org/10.1525/rep.2009.108.1.1.

4 See Carol Mastrangelo Bové, *Language and Politics in Julia Kristeva: Literature, Art, Therapy* (Albany, NY: SUNY Press, 2006), p. 5.

5 Julia Kristeva, "Colette," in *Female Genius: Life, Madness, Words—Hannah Arendt, Melanie Klein, Colette*, vol. 3, trans. Jane Marie Todd (New York: Columbia University Press, 2004).

6 Julia Kristeva, *"Ni Dépression ni perversion: l'éclosion Colette," Pulsions du temps* (Paris: Fayard, 2013), pp. 305–329; this essay first appeared as "Ni Dépression ni perversion: éclosion," in *l'Herne Colette*, ed. Gérard Bonal et Frédéric Maget (Paris: L'Herne, 2011), pp. 19–28.

7 Kristeva, *Colette*, 229–302.

8 See Christopher Caldwell, "Is This the End of French Intellectual Life?," *The New York Times* (March 5, 2021). https://www.nytimes.com/2021/03/05/opinion/french-intellectual-life-america.html?searchResultPosition=6.

9 Julia Kristeva, *"Colette,"* in *Le Génie féminin*. vol. 3 (Paris. Fayard, 2002); "Stabat Mater," in *Tales of Love*, trans. Leon Roudiez (New York: Columbia University Press,1987), pp. 234–264; *Powers of Horror*, trans. Leon Roudiez (New York: Columbia University Press, 1982), pp. 1–15.

10 Colette, *Chéri and The End of Chéri*, trans. Rachel Careau (New York: W.W. Norton & Co., 2022), Colette, *My Mother's House and Sido*, trans. Una Vicenzo Troubridge & Enid McLeod (New York: Farrar, Straus & Giroud, 2002), Colette, *Gigi, Julie De Carneilan*, and *Other Acquaintances: Three Short Novels*, trans. Roger Senhouse & Patrick Leigh Fermor (New York: Farrar, Straus & Giroud, 2001); *Gigi*, directed by Vincente Minnelli (Los Angeles County, CA: Studio Distribution Services, 2010), first appearing in 1958, DVD; *Colette*, directed by Wash Westmoreland (Santa Monica, CA: Lionsgate Home Entertainment, 2019), first appearing in 2018, DVD. All the following references use these texts, unless indicated otherwise.

11 See Julia Kristeva, *"Colette,"* in *Female Genius: Life, Madness, Words—Hannah Arendt, Melanie Klein, Colette*, vol. 3, trans. Jane Marie Todd (New York: Columbia University Press, 2004), p. 50.

12 See Paul-Claude Racamier, *L'Inceste et l'incestuel* (Paris: Dunod, 2021).

13 See RobertEpstein, S.D. Bock, M.J. Drew et al., "Infantilization Across the Life Span:A Large-Scale Internet Study Suggests That Emotional Abuse Is Especially Damaging," *Motivation and Emotion*, vol. 47 (2023): 137–163. https://doi.org/10.1007/s11031-022-09989-4.
14 Colette, *Break* of *Day,* trans. *Enid* McLeod (New York: Farrar, Straus & Giroud, 1979), p. 62.
15 *Chéri* and *The End of Chéri*, p. 61.
16 *Chéri* and *The End of Chéri*, p. 63.
17 *Chéri* and *The End of Chéri*, pp. 38–39.
18 See for example Lawrence Venuti, *The Translator's Invisibility: A History of Translation* (Oxford and New York: Routledge, 2008).
19 Bové, p. 136.
20 Colette, *My Mother's House and Sido*, p. 6.
21 Colette, *My Mother''s House and Sido*, p. 138.
22 Colette, "*La Maison de Claudine*," in *Œuvres*, vol. II, ed. Claude Pichois (Paris: Gallimard, 1986), p. 1082.
23 Jean Laplanche and Jean-Bertrand Pontalis, *The Language of Psychoanalysis*, trans. Donald Nicholson-Smith (New York:, Norton, 1973), p. 216n.
24 Simone de Beauvoir, "The Married Woman," in *The Second Sex*, trans. Constance Borde and Sheila Malovany-Chevallier (New York: Vintage, 2011), p. 445.
25 Colette, *Gigi*, p. 48.
26 Colette, *Gigi*, p. 58.
27 In addition to her book of 2002, *Colette*, p. 18, see Kristeva's *Time and Sense*, trans. Ross Guberman (New York: Columbia University Press, 1996), p. 269, where she discusses Maurice Merleau-Ponty's elaboration of the idea of "the flesh of the world."
28 Kristeva, *Colette*, p. 376.
29 Kristeva, *Colette*, pp. 316–317.
30 Jerry Aline Flieger, *Colette and the Fantom Subject of Autobiography* (Ithaca: Cornell University Press, 1992), pp. 48, 57.
31 Flieger, p. 127.
32 Kristeva, p. 351.
33 "Female Sexuality," in *The Standard Edition of the Complete Psychological Works of Sigmund Freud*, vol. 21 (London: Hogarth, 1953–73), pp. 223–243.
34 Flieger, p. 202.
35 Flieger, p. 2.

Chapter 1

A WOMAN OF A CERTAIN AGE: *CHÉRI*

Colette's biography and the social fabric of France in the early decades of the twentieth century are the ground from which *Chéri* (1920) emerges.[1] They do not, however, account for the force of the tragic, incestual, love story. She writes it before the development of the incestual affair between the forty-seven-year-old author and her seventeen-year-old stepson, Bertrand de Jouvenel. As Julia Kristeva puts it: "the fantasy truly preceded the act."[2] However, the rapport between Léa and Chéri does replay that of the author's first marriage with the sexes reversed. My concluding chapter on Wash Westmoreland's bio picture focuses on the significance of her first marriage in her writing including *Chéri*. Colette's infamous relationship with her husband, the forty-year-old Willy (Henry Gauthier-Villars), infantilized the nineteen-year-old young woman as well as enslaved and/or exploited her as a factory worker. He locked her up like a misbehaving child to force her to write and then published her work under his name.

While they do not discuss explicitly the incest taboo and the specific gendered behaviors analyzed below, Alex Hughes and Mary Noonan document the sexism of Belle Époque culture depicted in the narrative.[3] My analysis of the novel does not in itself reveal the way Colette portrays the patriarchal culture of her time. With evidence from these scholars, it does, however, make a compelling argument for the presence of the prohibition and gendered conduct in this period. Society considers the "parent–child" love affair taboo at the same time that the prohibition ironically enables said society to exist. While culture shapes her narrative, it does not deny the strength and invention of her portrayal of Léa and Chéri's tragic love story, which Frank Kermode names so well, but without reference to the hidden prohibition. He says, "With a great technical and moral leap [...]. Coletteinvents a mode, the mode of hedonist tragedy."[4] As *Chéri* makes clear, the taboo exists, even in its promiscuous courtesan environment.

The scene in which the young man kisses Léa for the first time followed by her embracing him and their lovemaking highlights the anxiety raised in her by this development. Formerly "too close a family friend, an indulgent godmother," she now becomes his lover. The narrator describes her during sex as "full of anxiety, as if she had unintentionally done him a very great wrong."[5] Negative and positive consequences ensue. In this case, the couple's happiness is at stake and vulnerable to the prohibition. Culture also works as a destructive force more generally in the background of the narrative, for instance, in Léa's life as a courtesan, despite its financial rewards. While it is possible to view her work as no worse than any other, it is more likely that having sex to earn one's living damages a woman's self-esteem and more generally her emotional and physical well-being. While Léa often appears confident and healthy before the momentous discovery of her feelings for Chéri, there is evidence of the harm her work has inflicted to the extent that at forty-seven, she has been unsuccessfully seeking a suitable and proper love object for many years and suffering from its lack.

A harmful element of the culture also appears in Chéri's silence, particularly concerning his emotions. The complex young man displays the masculine tendency often valued under patriarchy to be impassive, though Léa links the silence to his character. She intuits it in problematic terms as that of a stranger, "Chinese or Negro." One also reads this trait as an aspect of the universally perceived difficulty of understanding another person as in the case of Proust's youthful love object in *A la recherche du temps perdu*, Albertine. Chéri's androgynous qualities, also visible in the former, add to the complexity of Léa's young lover and to his vulnerability in the social order. The narrator documents the neglect of his biological mother, Madame Peloux, discussed below, as well as the damaging incestual relationship with Léa, examined throughout this chapter.

The positive results of the taboo for Chéri would enable the "child" to mature and assume his social role, that of a "père de famille." The prohibition prevents the debilitating guilt connected not only to violating the social contract but also to hurting others. More accurately, a feeling of culpability results from destabilizing the possibility of the social order and from causing Edmée to suffer. This suffering is thus another harmful result prevented by the taboo—Chéri's fiancée and later wife Edmée is the significant example here. Furthermore, the prohibition enables the individuals to avoid confronting the deterioration of the "parent's" body, not a negligible issue in an amorous relationship, particularly for Léa and many of Colette's characters who prize physical beauty so greatly.

Alex Hughes's "1900–1969: Writing the Void" helps to understand how the social shapes her writing in the period 1920–1930, especially *Chéri* and *The End of Chéri*. The analysis emphasizes the conservative patriarchal values as well as a crisis in masculine identity in the face of women's rising autonomy in post–WWI France. Léa's passion for Chéri would fly in the face of the period's gendered beliefs in keeping the status quo. As Mary Noonan points out in her analysis of the topic in this collection of essays, *A History of Women's Writing in France*, at the same time, there is a lampooning of the "new woman" in the French Press.

The relevance of the topics of incestual love and infantilization in Colette's writing goes beyond Hughes's and Noonan's focus on France. Shawn R. Smolen-Morton convincingly examines the actual transformation of adults into children, particularly in males, while I am focusing on unconscious formations in women's psychology in fiction and film—Colette's *Chéri* in this chapter. He also analyzes the phenomenon of infantilization in literature and movies in a way that reveals the relevance of this theme to power relations among people of all ages in a variety of times and places up to the present day, especially in the United States and Europe in 1935–1985.

Implicit in the tragic tale of Léa's "parenting" of and sexual relations with Chéri is the abuse of a child's mentality in the young lover, though he is biologically not a child. Colette implicitly raises the issue of pedophiliac behavior and its clear connections to parent–child relations in the couple's incestual longings and their responses, especially in Léa's confrontation and efforts to cope with it. The novelist's exploration of this problem enables a better understanding of such desires and their implications for power relations. They lead the reader to consider how to respond to such feelings, and question to what degree they may continue to lay at the root of abusive behavior and psychological instability in women, and more generally in individuals, couples, and larger groups.

Kristeva's understanding of the interaction between society and the individual implies that despite the force of the social pressures creating hurdles for women, it is possible to exercise free will and achieve a degree of autonomy. As examined below, her work dealing with this thorny issue, as well as with the ways in which Colette's writing incorporates "the flesh of the world," shapes my psychoanalytic reading of *Chéri*.

Chéri poses the problem of Colette's sense of "the catastrophe of love" in the form of an incestual relationship, a topic to which she will return more than once. Incestual desire in *Chéri*, however, as the term shows, is not for an object biologically related. Such an object appears both two years later, buried in the unconscious subtext of *La Maison de Claudine* (1922) (see my Chapter 2) and much later with some ambiguity in *Gigi* (1944, see Chapter 3). Other examples include her *Break of Day* (1928) and *The Pure and the Impure* (1932).

The central problem appearing in the earliest of the three novels examined in this book is whether Colette, via her narrative of Léa's plight, is confronting and coping with "the catastrophe of love" or escaping from it in writing incestual desire. The novel conveys the lovers' complex evolving psychology in which the reader at times finds both confrontation and escape: the unconscious fears and desires of both Léa and Chéri as they grow more aware of their love and of the responsibility for infantilizing the young lover. They also experience increasingly oppressive culpability over the suffering they are inflicting on Edmée. Furthermore, in loving him, the protagonist suffers as well from the inevitable aging of her body. Painfully aware of these physical changes, Léa comes to understand that she loves Chéri and that she must free him to pursue his life as a man and not a child. The third-person-limited narrator creates a young man who is difficult to decipher but there is evidence of his concomitant growing awareness of stunted growth and the part he plays in the negative and positive consequences of their passion.

Colette's narrative reveals the conflicted psychology of her characters, especially of Léa, as they engage in incestual love. The novel makes clear how incestuous desire destabilizes the social contract and also reveals their increasing awareness of the source of their psychological distress in the face of a society without order. My thesis focuses on the question of whether the text portrays Colette's confrontation and coping with the taboo—this is the more probable interpretation given the textual evidence, as I am arguing—or instead her attempt to escape it.

The novel's revelation of the protagonists' psychology emphasizes the dangers and bouts of anxiety going with the choice to follow incestual desire, as an analysis of important excerpts uncovers in this chapter. The early passage on the theme in "Introduction" above identified the unconscious affect in Léa's response to her lover's impending marriage.

Not only had Chéri been unable to verbalize his positive and negative feelings toward his love but also—more significant in my examination of women's psychology in Colette—Léa had unsurmountable difficulties in expressing her own emotions and thoughts. Kristeva's theory on abjection is relevant here in that the inability to use language is a symptom of this state of mind, which goes beyond the more general sense of serious depression.[6] In the struggle to acquire language, children separate from their mother and develop a relationship with the father, ideally one that is nurturing—the father of individual or personal prehistory, as described in Freud.[7] Here, Léa and Chéri regress in their incestual rapport, replaying that earlier struggle and confronting difficulty in articulating their thoughts and feelings.

As mentioned earlier, Colette is also rehearsing her relationship with Willy, reversing the child/parent roles to have Léa take on the mother's part in her interactions with Chéri. Wash Westmoreland's film focuses on the novelist's struggle to speak truth to power in her first marriage.

In *Chéri*, Colette conveys their visceral response to the marriage via the third-person-limited narrator's subtle commentary revealing the couple's inarticulate state. In a later flashing back, the novelist continues to emphasize their difficulty in expressing themselves in words and conveys the partly unconscious passion of the two in their first sexual encounter at Chéri's home prior to their trip to Normandy. Once again, the narrator communicates their sensations and feelings including desires and fears of which they are not fully aware. On this occasion, it is not in connection with the upcoming marriage as in the earlier passage but with their passion for each other more directly. They do no more than kiss twice on the lips but in doing so Léa experiences a love unlike none other in her life—filling a lack that has been painful. Chéri confirms that he feels the same.

Colette sets up the encounter by stressing the spontaneous, unintentional drawing together of the two while Chéri's mother is present, thus contrasting very different "mothers." Despite the harmful elements of the protagonist's motherly love, she is less abusive than the unintelligent biological mother who has neglected her son since birth. Here, Madame Peloux feels resentment each time Chéri's cheek moves close to Léa's neck. After his mother leaves, Léa enjoys his warm breath on her ear, drawing him near her "without any ulterior motive" (27).[8] The narrative conveys the complexity of their feelings and thoughts, which include and go beyond desire. There is a longing for companionship, for instance, in Chéri's repeated reference to Léa as his "buddy" ("un frère"). The text also communicates the dimensions of their rapport in her admiration for his articulate comment on the beautiful perfume entering the bedroom—rare though such remarks are from this young man who is so often silent.

Chéri's words introduce the idea of "a child's" precious imagination into the narrative of incestual longing in Colette's writing. This reference will become especially strong in *La Maison de Claudine*. In other words, the author values to a high degree the ability of children to think creatively, free of the social limitations later imposed on them. This idea helps to explain the fascination of the incest taboo in her writing, given that a "child" is an active participant in relationships engaging in prohibited longings. Here, Chéri's observation of the smell of the acacia blooms having consumed the orange blossoms not only has Léa admire his words but also appropriately conveys the "child's" imagination and the strength of their problematic passion, which has aroused their lovemaking. The narrator points out that the perfume is so strong that they both turn in the same instant to look at its source in the window. His comment—an example of Colette's powerful writing—that the acacia with pink blooms, drinking the orange blossom on this evening, also subtly connotes Léa's enjoying Chéri. The novel, from its beginning, associates pink with the courtesan, for instance, in the description of her bedroom. Their incestual love echoes in the perfume breathed by the young man, in the text's words, the "willing victim."

Furthermore, Colette emphasizes the physical force of this love after the second kiss in Chéri's murmuring and moaning "an entire tender, animal song." I will return to the importance of such images in the discussion of the author's pets to convey the "child's" lack of autonomy in my concluding chapter. Here, she also has the narrator describe Léa's encounter with him several times as intuiting both that it is sublime and then that it is not good, as the following quotations reveal, respectively: "the brilliance of his suddenly reopened eyes unsettled Léa like an abruptly switched-on light" (27); "he murmured [...] a song that she listened to bent over him and full of anxiety, as if she had unintentionally done him a very great wrong" (30). The episode makes clear that this is a critical moment in the relationship. Léa and Chéri are in the murky process of coming to understand what the unconscious hides. Colette has the narrator introduce it with "One June evening [...] altered the destinies of the young man and the mature woman" (24).

A final passage dramatizes at length and, in detail, the couple's wrenching decision to separate. After demonstrating Léa's ecstatic joy in welcoming back her lover, Colette describes her anticipation of their reunion in sex with the phrase "the most terrifying joy of her life," conveying both the strength of her passion and fear, suggesting the recently earned awareness that it is wrong. Seeming to forget that awareness, she comes to embrace not only Chéri but also the renewal of their love as inevitable and good. She begins to organize with enthusiasm their getaway to the South to enjoy their companionship in tranquility.

Such moments problematize the overall sense that Colette is confronting and coping with incestual desire. The text depicts an unrealistic unconscious fantasy, which ignores the reality of their unwise relationship, as one sees in Léa's excessively energetic effort to plan their train trip. Chéri, however, more lucid in these final pages in acknowledging their harmful behavior, brings Léa to her senses by observing that if he is acting "like a twelve-year old," it is because he is with her, "With you, Nounou, I would very likely remain twelve years old for half a century."

Even more significantly in reawakening her understanding, when she speaks harshly of Edmée, he refers to her former better self, including the goodness and kindness of her nature in the past, for instance, in considering his wife. In keeping with the up-and-down rhythms, which their relationship has experienced since the opening of the novel revealing the news of Chéri's impending marriage, the fluctuating cadence of the concluding pages moves the tragedy to its final stage. Colette's ability to write dynamic prose is evident in this rhythm. It is true that her plots in themselves are not noteworthy for their action. Pierre Schneider in fact calls them banal, while praising her depiction of characters struggling with the conflict between thought and animality.[9] There is a great deal of movement, however, in the final pages of this novel, generated by the intense physical and psychological agitation of Chéri, and especially of Léa. Here, in the novel's final pages, Chéri's, and especially Léa's, intense physical and psychological agitation generates a great deal of movement. The dynamic qualities of her prose, which my Introduction describes as cadenced, rhythmic recurrences of departures and returns are evident throughout *Chéri*. Léa perceives in a glimpse of her lover as he leaves her courtyard that, like an escaping prisoner, the young man will be free of the dangerous parent–child affair with the mature woman. Colette makes clear that it is only in the very end that Léa fully acknowledges the import of their familial rapport, both its value and its destructiveness. Does she, however, choose separation or accept it because of Chéri's observations? In other words, would she have allowed the continuation of the damaging relationship without his intervention? The latter behavior would be an escape from the reality of her/their desire. Thus, Colette's depiction of Chéri's departure, like that of a criminal fleeing prison, serves also to have the reader reflect on Léa's ambiguous behavior as she responds to his leaving. The reference to her glimpsing herself in the mirror as a madwoman emphasizes the recognition of the ambiguities of their behavior, particularly of her role as a "bad mother."

These pages display Colette's writing at its best, bringing to life the intense emotions and sensations of the protagonists, the volatility of their relationship, their competitiveness, and the combination of unconscious drive as well as growing awareness of the stakes of their problematic rapport. Léa says both "I love you" and "It's too late."[10] Earlier on, Colette had introduced this volatile Léa at her wits end dealing with Chéri's departure: she unsuccessfully engages in distracting and relaxing activities like walking, smoking, and eating to deal with her keen sense of loss. We read the details of her trying to find the right outfits including hiker's clothing as she tries a long walk only to change clothing out of fear that Chéri may see her on the street in this unflattering garb. Such scenes are further evidence of Colette's ability as a modernist novelist to use a sequence of departures and arrivals to have the reader feel the intensity of the characters' agitation as they grapple with incestual desire.

Once Chéri returns, they exchange volatile remarks, for example, his jealous accusations of clients and Léa's irritated comment that he has returned at midnight without consulting her. She works hard to appear indifferent and not at his command while in fact being overjoyed at his return. The description of her responding in monosyllables at one point as if asleep highlights a degree of unconscious affect in the scene: "as if she were hearing a sleeper speak in a dream" (131).

The novel overall conveys the complexity of Léa's psychology, especially as she both intuits her love and acknowledges it more consciously, by having the narrator reveal her interior monologues in quotation marks. In a scene prior to the conclusion, after Charlotte Peloux visits and expresses joy at her son's return to his wife after leaving for three months, for instance, we read such a description of the protagonist's thoughts and feelings, among the most telling: "My poor Chéri [...] we've lost the most honorable thing that we possessed on earth [...]." (119). In these words, the author conveys her sense that love, including incestual feeling, is indeed majestic as well as disturbing, a conviction to which she returns in the conclusion of *La Maison de Claudine.*

A complex Colette manages to communicate not only Léa's psyche but also Chéri's, revealing how a couple's identities may overlap and separate. In fact, as the following will prove in my continuing analysis in this book of Kristeva's insight into her writing, she identifies with certain male characters, including Chéri in this novel.[11]

While Léa has become aware of the nobility of their love for each other without saying so in the scene described above, in the final pages, he openly reveals his admiration for her noble humanity, for example, in her concern for and generosity toward Edmée. They perceive their relationship as arguably their most precious possession not only for its exquisite pleasures but also for its broader implications for the ethical treatment of self, each other, and the individuals who surround them, despite the contradictions. They have, for instance, acknowledged the stunting of Chéri's growth as a man and the suffering they cause Edmée.

In her approach to literature, Kristeva implicitly affirms the psyche's agency vis-à-vis the limits and opportunities afforded by society. In other words, human beings have the power, limited though it may be, to shape the social. The link between the two, however, is problematic, as Maria Margaroni points out in her analysis of Kristeva's theory.[12] The problem stems from not paying sufficient attention to material and historical conditions in interpreting the text's presentation of the dyad psyche/society. Despite this issue, informed by Kristeva's theory, my reading of *Chéri*, *La Maison de Claudine*, and *Gigi* also affirms literature's strengths in questioning truths and beliefs and thus in shaping the world via the mentality of its readers. Alice Jardine's biography of Kristeva is helpful in its examination of this complex relationship. She analyzes it in the context of the psychoanalytic writer's theory of the psychic interdependence of "the need to believe" and the "desire to know." In this novel, emotions and sensations (Léa's love for Chéri), as well as reason (her understanding of society and its contract), interact in the protagonist—the first constituting "the need to believe," the second, "the desire to know." These two poles shape the courtesan's words and behavior in the confrontation with incestual desire.

The novel portrays this link in a way that reveals the ability of human beings to act freely in the face of challenging obstacles posed by their environment, especially the incest taboo, as well as gender and age prejudice. In this context, Léa is a woman with considerable agency who exercises free will despite the passion she feels for Chéri and the social pressure on her as a woman to conform.

Colette's biography calls this reading into question, especially the degree to which she creates a protagonist able to make informed decisions and act on them in dealing with the unequal power dynamic in her relationship with Chéri. Kristeva's in-depth study of her life and work conveys an ambiguous stance toward politics, especially in the public domain. Her *Colette* reveals that she did not consider herself knowledgeable enough to comment on political life. She also did not speak out against the Vichy government's collaboration with Hitler until her third husband, Maurice Goudeket, a Jew, was threatened. That is to say, the author's words and behavior outside of the novels indirectly argue against her work as politically informed, concerning public and governmental relations. Her novels nonetheless reveal a keen understanding of personal power relations, especially in the demi-monde of early twentieth-century France, and an admirable talent for depicting them in the psychology and parent–child rapport between Léa and Chéri. Furthermore, other references to public political life show her knowledge of such affairs, for instance, the affectionate critique of her father's attempts to become a local deputy and even mayor of Saint Sauveur in *La Maison de Claudine*. The narrator is aware of the need for insight into the sincerity of supporters and one's opponents in the political domain.[13]

Julia Kristeva's theories on the dyad psyche/society and her insightful extensive analysis of Colette's writing as constituting "the flesh of the world" recognize the complexity, contradictions, and relevance of her novel beyond the issue of its public politics. Her study of both Léa's and Chéri's perspectives is not without its revelations of the problematic power dynamics of couples and families today. My focus here is on the key phrase "the flesh of the world" in her analysis, which is both thought-provoking and enigmatic as shown in my Introduction. To what degree is the world a material/physical entity "flesh"? Is it not also and primarily a social construction? The questions are relevant to my thesis on the problem Colette's writing poses in *Chéri*: how does one respond to and cope with incestual desire? According to Kristeva, her novels offer a unique verbal representation of sensual experience as "the world," including its objects and persons. If the social contract prohibits certain forms of that experience, namely the incestual, in what sense does the novel stand for such behavior as milieu, in other words, as existence in a social environment, "the flesh of the world"? *Chéri* emphasizes the ambiguities of Colette's response to forbidden love. In depicting the fluctuating variations in Léa's behavior between escape and confrontation, is Colette underlining the human need to conform to the social contract or to seek pleasure and flaunt the law? Her emphasis in the novel also suggests a third reading, a compromise between the two needs: to pursue the relationship for a time until the biological clock limits its duration as the couple, especially Léa, ages.

I have discussed the relevance of Heidegger's analysis of existence in the world to Kristeva's sense of Colette's writing as a transformation of that experience into a literary text. As I show in my *Kristeva in America: Re-imagining the Exceptional,* she locates some of the philosophical foundations of her work in Heidegger's reading of Kant. Freedom, she says, is the human capacity to question endlessly and forcefully, rather than to respond to and/or acquiesce to exterior forces, especially the marketplace.[14] Such questioning engages one in confronting the Other both within and outside of the psyche. In this context, I see Colette's *Chéri* as an example of such a confrontation in its compelling narrative of incestual desire, though not without ambiguity.

In Time and Sense, Kristeva also mentions a connection to Maurice Merleau-Ponty's elaboration of the very term "the flesh of the world."[15] His phenomenology, especially his late work on what has popularly come to be known as "the mind-body problem," is in keeping with Colette's thinking in *Chéri.* For Merleau-Ponty, literary language engages one in the "flesh of the world" at least in part because it constitutes a physical process in which one speaks and is also spoken to.[16] *Chéri* in this context is a visceral interaction between an individual in love and the world, understood as persons and objects—a material presence or milieu and a social contract including its prohibitions. A clear example of the novel as such an interplay between a person and the world (its "flesh" represented in the give-and-take of a couple) lies in the overlapping and separation between Léa and her young lover. The novel unfolds to reveal both of their perspectives as they acknowledge the ambiguous status of their passion as a possession that is precious and harmful at the same time. In other words, their words uncover not only individual psyches but also constitute a figure conveying the desire of two persons, as well as the social inhibitions pressing upon them—in this sense, "the flesh of the world." The novel recreates the experience of living viscerally in one's environment, presciently pointing to a topic prominent in recent literary studies, literature and the body, for instance, in the work of Hortense Spillers, RA Judy, and Sara Ahmed.[17]

As Kristeva makes clear in her essay included in this volume, Colette's recreation of physical and psychic experience in *Chéri* emerges out of incestuous/incestual desire and is grounded in presence, temporal unity, and I would add, memory.[18] Yet, her recreation also incorporates the strangeness of the Other (both internal and external) in its subject. In other words, her novel depicts "the flesh of the world" in the reciprocal exchange of words between Chéri and Léa, a dialogue that engages the reader in a consideration of distinct positions, including the lovers' passion and society's condemnation of it. The variety of perspectives is both material and historical, linking multiple moments and places. Furthermore, given that Kristeva shows evidence of Colette's identifications with Chéri as well as with the more obvious Léa, it becomes clear that the different positions incorporated in her writing include herself as a stranger, in other words, as possessing multiple identities, both feminine and masculine.

Michael Lucey has also pointed out Merleau-Ponty's relevance to Colette's writing. In discussing her first-person narrator and same-sex identity, he notes the connections both writers make between "I" and "one," including the spatial and temporal ramifications of these links. First-person narrators are figural and enable an author to express what would otherwise be without a voice. They make it possible to move beyond an individual situated only in one moment and place. While Colette employs a third-person-limited narrator in *Chéri*, the frequent insertions of Léa's monologues in quotation marks bridge the gap between "I" and "one" that Merleau-Ponty examines according to Lucey. Such monologues support his thesis founded in part on *Phenomenology and Perception* that a figure gives voice to desires inhibited by society.[19]

In an analysis giving far less attention than Lucey to the nuances, ambiguities, and methods of the texts as literature, Robin James has a very different take on Kristeva's reading of Colette's novels as writing which constitutes "the flesh of the world."[20] In a discussion of aesthetics, gender, and race, he claims that the French Bulgarian's theories underlying her interpretation exploit animals by appropriating their bodies in a way that denies their rights and dignity in order to serve the author's white privilege. James writes that "Kristeva's word choice reveals that her discussion of Colette's sensory "genius" is framed in obvious and objectionable colonial tropes."[21] He selects examples and claims to show that Colette's rehabilitation of the sensuous within writing poses "a challenge to the universe of *civilized mastery attributed to humans*" (Kristeva 12, emphasis mine) because it "can be read as *exquisite or troubling dehumanization*" (Kristeva 105, emphasis again mine). Here, he simplistically misinterprets both Colette and Kristeva's psychoanalytic reading of her novels.

It is true that Colette often uses animals to convey the physical force of emotions and sensations, for example, in describing Léa's passion for Chéri. The context of her writing and Kristeva's theory and criticism in *Colette*, however, prove that they are not appropriating the nonhuman bodily strength of animals as part of a cultural war to support white hegemony. Instead, they understand such physical force as part of the human experience, particularly in women's struggle with incestual/incestuous desire, as I argue in this book. Colette, according to Kristeva, challenges mastery, but not in the sense James understands, that the author exploits animal physicality to create an art that will redress Western forms lacking bodily force.

Instead, in *Colette's* reading of the novelist, she incorporates the semiotic in her writing in such a way that she confronts the mastery of symbolic language. Furthermore, the dehumanizing consequences of passion, such as that experienced by Léa, are both *exquisite and troubling*, as suggested in the French Bulgarian's analysis of the author's narratives taken as a whole. In other words, Colette, as Kristeva understands, portrays the pleasure and guilt resulting from incestual desire. She writes, "The metaphoric body, for its part, is not unaware of that logic [Oedipal], but unrepentantly incestuous, it also does not stop there [...]. More than a *pleasure* with precise objects as its aim, it is the *joy* that overflows and excenters them: that ek-static jubilation lies behind a poetics of the fragment in which the union with a torrent and that with a woman, a man, or a cat assume the same importance."[22] It is clear that in analyzing Colette's metaphoric body, in other words, her paradoxical body as incorporated in her writing, Kristeva describes the drama of love, which the author conveys so well, rather than an exploitative use of animals. As Pierre Schneider says:

> Indeed few writers have illustrated more poignantly the definition of humans as thinking animals. The animal world *was* Colette's world: she wrote superbly about the cats, the dogs that were her companions. She lived too under a constant bombardment of incredibly sharp, diverse and intense sensual data. To render these was her task—a task seemingly insurmountable, for the senses function at close range while words operate at a distance. Yet, of all of Colette's marriages, this mating of senses and speech was the least likely and the most successful.

Without mentioning incestual desire, Schneider not only points to her love for her pets but also both the similarity and difference between humans and animals. Rather than exploiting them, she writes in a way that recognizes their power in enabling her to convey that strength in words, which, at the same time, transforms physical experience into a struggle to understand prohibitions.[23]

Jerry Flieger's analysis of the complex female protagonist also shows the central problem of illicit desire in *Chéri*,[24] although her conclusions inadequately recognize the strength of the author's writing in certain of her novels including this one. Her book on Colette is valuable both, in general, as a model of psychoanalytic reading with some theory and more particularly for its close readings of the novels. She sees Léa as an object of desire and as an authority figure. Flieger's understanding of Léa's complexity points to the ambiguities of the novel vis-à-vis incestual longings. The courtesan represents sensual pleasure for herself and Chéri at the same time as she is the ethical figure who in the end rejects infantilizing her young lover and abusing his wife. As I have pointed out, Colette problematizes that rejection by making clear Chéri's role in having his mature lover come to her senses, ironically enough.

Flieger's *Colette and the Fantom Subject of Autobiography*, particularly its conclusions, gives no less attention to the form than to the content of Colette's writing and recognizes its contributions to modernist literature, using the terms "modernity" and "moderns."[25] In *Chéri*, these include non-straight protagonists in the young lover as well as cadenced or rhythmic recurrences of departures and returns, as I have noted.

Flieger's conclusions, however, do not all ring true. She faults Colette in such novels as *Chéri* for anger, melancholy, and self-recrimination. One sees this especially in Léa. In my reading, *Chéri* gives evidence of the dread attending passion and of the "messiness of experience," in a way that brings about reflection on the difficult choices open to women in the struggle with incestual/incestuous desire. For this reason, I believe, it is her best novel. Flieger's faulting of Colette in such narratives inadvertently calls attention to the strengths of her writing. As I read it, her writing movingly dramatizes the range of emotions, sensations, and behaviors in a woman's challenging confrontation with passion and, in *Chéri*, the infantilizing of a young lover.

Notes

1 Colette, *Chéri and The End of Chéri*, trans. Rachel Careau (New York: W.W. Norton & Co., 2022).

2 Julia Kristeva, *Colette, in Female Genius: Life, Madness, Words—Hannah Arendt, Melanie Klein, Colette*, vol. 3, trans. Jane Marie Todd (New York: Columbia University Press, 2004), p. 52.

3 See Alex Hughes's "1900–1969: Writing the Void," and Mary Noonan's "Voicing the Feminine: French Women Playwrights of the Twentieth Century," in *A History of Women's Writing in France*, ed. Sonya Stephens (Cambridge: Cambridge University Press, 2000), pp. 147–167 and 220–235, respectively.

4 See Frank Kermode, "Colette: Review of *The Blue Lantern*." *The New Yorker*, vol. 1, no. 8 (December 12, 1963). https://www-nybooks-com.pitt.idm.oclc.org/articles/1963/12/12/colette/.

5 Colette, pp. 24, 30.

6 See Julia Kristeva, *Powers of Horror*, trans. Leon Roudiez (New York: Columbia University Press, 1982), p. 13.
7 See Sigmund Freud, *Group Psychology and the Analysis of the Ego*, trans. and ed. James Strachey (New York: Norton, 1959), p. 33.
8 Colette, p. 27.
9 See Pierre Schneider, "Paris: Fresh Look at Colette's Work," *The New York Times* (April 9, 1973). https://archive.nytimes.com/www.nytimes.com/books/99/10/17/specials/colette-fresh.html.
10 Colette, p. 150.
11 Kristeva, *Colette*, p. 178.
12 See the discussion of Margaroni on this topic in my *Kristeva in America: Re-Imagining the Exceptional* (New York: Palgrave, 2020), p. 45; see also her "Recent Work on and by Julia Kristeva: Toward a Psychoanalytic Social," *Signs*, vol. 32, no. 3, (Spring, 2007): 793–808.
13 Colette, *My Mother's House*, in *My Mother's House and Sido*, trans. Una Vicenzo [sic] Troubridge and Enid McLeod (New York: Farrar, Straus and Giroux LLC, 1981) p. 40.
14 See my *Kristeva in America: Re-Imagining the Exceptional*, p. 49, on her essay "Europhilia-Europhobia," in *Intimate Revolt*, trans. Jeanine Herman (New York: Columbia University Press, 2002), pp. 255–268.
15 *Time and Sense*, trans. Ross Guberman (New York: Columbia University Press, 1996), p. 269.
16 See Maurice Merleau-Ponty, *The Visible and the Invisible*, trans. Alphonso Lingis (Evanston, Il: Northwestern University Press, 1968), pp. 138–139.
17 Hortense Spillers, "Mama's Baby, Papa's Maybe: An American Grammar Book," *Diacritics*, vol. 17, no. 2 (1987): 65–81. *JSTOR*, https://doi.org/10.2307/464747. Accessed March 31, 2023; Sara Ahmed. *Queer Phenomenology: Orientations, Objects, Others* (Durham, NC: Duke University Press, 2006); R. A. Judy. *Sentient Flesh: Thinking in Disorder, Poiesis in Black.* (Duke University Press, 2020). https://doi.org/10.1215/9781478012559.
18 Julia Kristeva, "Ni dépression, ni perversion: éclosion," in *l'Herne Colette*, eds. Gérard Bonal et Frédéric Maget (Paris: L'Herne, 2011), pp. 19–28.
19 See Michael Lucey, *Never Say I: Sexuality and the First Person in Colette, Gide, and Proust* (Durham, NC: Duke, 2006). Kindle, p. 163.
20 See Robin James, "From receptivity to transformation: on the intersection of race, gender, and the aesthetic in contemporary continental philosophy" in *Convergences: Black Feminism and Continental Philosophy*, eds. Kathryn Gines, Donna-Dale Marcano & Maria Davidson (Albany, NY: SUNY Press, 2010), pp. 135–156. https://philarchive.org/rec/JAMFRT.
21 James, p. 141.
22 Julia Kristeva, *Colette*, pp. 198–199.
23 See Pierre Schneider, "Paris: Fresh Look at Colette's Work." https://archive.nytimes.com/www.nytimes.com/books/99/10/17/specials/colette-fresh.html.
24 Jerry Aline Flieger, *Colette and the Fantom Subject of Autobiography* (Ithaca: Cornell University Press, 2002).
25 Flieger, p. 2.

Chapter 2

LA MAISON DE CLAUDINE: MAMAN NOT CLAUDINE

This chapter examines the long-misunderstood 1922 novel focused not on the character Claudine but on Colette's mother as a key to her writing and its pervasive incest taboo. The misleading title—the result of the author's and publisher's desire to capitalize on the series' popularity—is not the primary reason for the misunderstanding at the heart of the narrative, as I will explain. This close reading of *La Maison de Claudine* shows for the first time how the metaphors of sewing and the voice link the narrator, mother, daughter, and gay actor, gradually revealing how the desire for the maternal figure poses serious challenges for self-knowledge and psychological health. In unrelated episodes, especially those dealing with these characters, Sido, Bel-Gazou, and Marcel d'Avricourt, Colette probes the conflicts arising from sexual drives both straight and gay.

While Julia Kristeva's *Colette* is an exception, earlier scholarship as well as the commonplace view of the novel, for example, on blogs such as those of WordPress, fail to acknowledge the threat posed by such conflicts, distorting it as a nostalgic, idyllic recreation of a happy childhood.[1] This includes that of the brilliant novelist Doris Lessing in her forward to Andrew Brown's uneven translation published by Hesperus in 2005.[2] Here, I explode most earlier interpretations with special emphasis on a female psychology very different from that identified by Lessing as well as by other critics whose take on the novel as idealized memories is similar. While it is true that Colette celebrates to a considerable extent the mother figure Sido especially and also the daughter who vividly conveys the precious imagination of the child, the novel as a whole stages a complex confrontation with illicit drives, particularly the incest taboo, a drama missing in the criticism.

This interpretation led to my new, forthcoming translation, which in turn contributed to discoveries confirming my sense of the novel. A careful reading of the original uncovers the incest taboo and a bisexual voice central to the spirit of *La Maison de Claudine.* My goal was to recreate it in my tongue. Though serious discussion of translation is infrequent in criticism of world literature given into English, such analysis can provide vital knowledge as in this case.

The theoretical context for the recent version, based on work in the emerging field of translation studies, emphasizes the changing historical conditions, which shape the rendering of a text into a different language. These include the translator's culture, formation, and research, as well as the understanding of translation as a hermeneutic process and an unconscious language.

My effort in this chapter is to uncover the spirit of the original French's long-overlooked buried subtext of bisexuality and incestuous desire.[3] I bring together here the results of my years' long study of the novel honed in the library and classroom. The chapter and previously published essays[4] dealing with the translation of Colette are based on my version of the 117-page novel as it appears in the most reliable edition, that of the Pléiade. The previous translators to which I refer are Una Vincenzo Troubridge and Enid McLeod as well as Andrew Brown.[5]

While I applaud these translations in the attention they give to Colette's remarkable novel and in fact have found them useful in producing my own, serious weaknesses exist. Troubridge and McLeod, in what is probably the most read edition, omit six chapters in the definitive version dealing with animals, a topic central to the novelist's depiction of the human being as a thinking animal.[6] Brown's is uneven, for example, translating "father" for "frère" in the chapter "Toutouque" (86). My translation, including chapters missing in the Troubridge/McLeod version, makes clear what earlier English versions do not: that the apparently neutral presentation of heterosexuality filters the incestuous voice of the bisexual narrator and author.

Colette published the novel's chapters as separate pieces dealing with her childhood. Later, she revised and collected them, creating a complex autobiographical narrative in which intriguing metaphors like that of sewing link disparate sections, as I will show. Literary critics recognize the text's formal classification as a novel whose coherence derives from the theme of childhood. The subtext of bisexuality and the way the author expresses it, however, have gone unrecognized. They created a fundamental unity and broke ground in 1922 as an unorthodox early experiment in literary modernism. The strength of so many of the chapters to stand on their own sometimes leads to their treatment as short stories. I in fact have taught them as a novel in my "Women and Literature" class and as short stories in a course on that genre at the University of Pittsburgh.

Balancing a careful close reading of the original with a rendering that is proper for an English-speaking audience in 2024, I have made choices based on the French, on the target audience, and also on my formation and research as a psychoanalytic reader of world literature. While for some theorists, especially prior to the emergence of translation studies as a discipline, an invisible translator makes the original text transparent in a second language, I maintain in line with recent research that this is not the case. The gendered, psychoanalytic character of the original text calls upon the reader of Colette in a different tongue to play a significant artistic role in hearing and revealing it. In this translation, *La Maison de Claudine* gives literary expression to a psychic formation, desire for the mother, which is a creative and healthy confrontation with the status quo. This is not to say that Colette condones incest but rather that she implicitly raises questions about the taboo and how to respond to it rather than repress it as is often the case. I refer to Kristeva's take on the novelist's confrontation with incest in her article, "Ni Depression ni perversion: l'éclosion," in English translation appearing for the first time in this volume.[7] Informed by her analyses in that article and her book on the author, I go beyond her take, examining significant passages from my translation to illustrate Colette's innovative modernist aesthetic and its hidden voicing of incestuous desire.

In *La Maison de Claudine*, Colette reveals the historical and political conditions of her life as a bisexual woman in early twentieth-century France. I see the text as modernist feminist fiction, inventing the characteristics of the genre appearing at the time in Virginia Woolf's *Mrs. Dalloway* and other groundbreaking novels by women: time-shifts, dreams, and word plays, for instance. Most importantly, as I demonstrate in my readings of such texts in *Language and Politics in Julia Kristeva* when I first examined it, *La Maison de Claudine* incorporates another attribute of modernism, an unconventional female character's perspective.[8] Colette and her narrator subvert middle-class customs and the incest taboo deriving from the monotheism and male God which establish conduct considered "normal." Such behavior dictates that a woman be monogamous and married, or else marginalized, for example, as a prostitute.

Simone de Beauvoir recognized Colette's *La Maison de Claudine* as a significant rethinking of patriarchy and heterosexuality in the chapter on "The Married Woman" in *The Second Sex* in 1949.[9] This important early recognition of the novel's critique of normative gender and sexuality calls attention to the need for the re-examination of Colette's modernist text. The controversy surrounding the translation of Beauvoir's foundational text in women's studies also shows the necessity to examine problems in the English versions of *La Maison de Claudine*. Such study enables an appreciation of the contributions of creative writers, especially in re-evaluating the translated works by canonical women artists and their psychology in a world in which gendered assumptions are in flux and such re-evaluations of translations are rare.

Beyond the fact of my formation (in French literature) and research (in Neo-Freudian literary criticism), a psychoanalytic reading is highly appropriate and productive given the particular characteristics of this novel and the way in which it contributes to knowledge on women's psychology as I will demonstrate. My Introduction above points out the striking parallels to Freud's groundbreaking work in Colette's, as both Kristeva and Flieger prove. An important example in which *La Maison de Claudine* comes closest to revealing the conviction that all humans are bisexual persons appears in the passage on "that most majestic and disturbing of drives" (my translation) when read in context.[10]

La Maison de Claudine depicts a stereotypical female icon, the home, in the sometimes seemingly unrelated everyday events occurring in a Burgundian village. The narrator lovingly describes her mother as an intelligent, strong-willed, honest, and generous woman devoted to her family, dogs, cats, and books. The daughter tells the story of her mother's life from her marriage to the Burgundian property-owner who "kidnapped" her away from her bohemian brothers living in Belgium, to her second marriage to Captain Colette, and finally, to her feisty old age and demise.

A critique of heterosexuality and an unconscious desire for a person of the same sex or a gay person of a different sex underlies the discourse from the beginning. The mother is the earliest object of desire, for example, in episodes from the first half of the novel including the opening chapter, "Où sont les enfants?" ("Where are the Children?") and "La Petite" ("Little One"). The title of the first is her mother's repeated question as she looks for her children in these memories of a pleasurable and protective home. "La Petite" introduces the mother and her thimble, illuminated in the window of her home, making clear that she embodies what is most critical to the narrator/daughter's sense of who she is. Remembering arouses a sense of guilt, however, in the narrator/daughter because, in growing up and becoming part of Parisian life, she has become less like her mother, and because of the incestuous element in the daughter's longings. Colette's biography no doubt contributes to this feeling of culpability: at the age of forty-seven, she engages in an incestuous affair with her sixteen-year-old stepson, Bertrand de Jouvenel during the time she writes this novel. He says that he urged her to write it after their visit to her birthplace in 1922.This emotion permeates the novel, linking the mother to the gay actor Marcel and her daughter Bel-Gazou as I will show.

In this context, the novel is in fact a critique of heterosexuality in the form of a language of desire for the mother as a visceral, gay experience and a politics. The union of narrator and mother in such chapters as "Jalousie" ("Jealousy"), along with the negative portrayal of heterosexual behavior in, for example, "Le Sauvage" ("The Savage"), combine to create a bisexual subtext requiring a new and more adequate translation. Examples from the beginning, middle, and end of the novel ("Jalousie," "Mode de Paris" ("Rage of Paris"), and "La Couseuse" ("The Sempstress"), respectively) demonstrate how the new translation recreates the French version more adequately, particularly in rendering the subtext of incest and bisexuality.

I am arguing that a sexual code, especially in references to such gendered signifiers as sewing, the voice, and the eyes in "The Rage of Paris" and throughout the book reveals Colette's unconscious longings. Recreating this increasingly open language of sexuality, as I understand it building on Kristeva's take,[11] my translation illuminates the novel's meanings, which would otherwise remain disconnected and unexplained. Pleasure, fear, a violation of the norms, silence, and guilt, as in the narrator's pervasive sense that she no longer deserves the world that her mother stands for, or at least its memory,[12] are among the characteristics it brings to her fiction. In this context, the mother functions as an object of desire, enabling Colette to raise the question of how to live one's sexuality in 1922, a question with ethical implications that continues to resonate to this day given the persistence of homophobia and incestuous/incestual relations in many countries including France and the United States.

The chapter "The Rage of Paris" is the strongest evidence of the novel's bisexual subtext insufficiently conveyed in the earlier translations. This is the episode in which the chateau owner returns home to find his wife and other townspeople including men engaged in embroidering sessions with the seductive young actor Marcel. Here and throughout the novel Colette uses the image of sewing, especially needles and pins, as well as the sound of the voice, to connect the mother, daughter Bel-Gazou, and Marcel to the narrator in ways that highlight the latter's bisexuality and incestuous desire.

The portrait of Marcel is one of those unrelated digressions mentioned earlier only loosely connected to the story in that he is part of the narrator's life in the Burgundian village, Saint-Sauveur-en-Puisaye, for a brief time. His presence is striking for the narrator, unaccustomed to such talented, attractive actors in her small town. As the chapter unfolds, his mysterious seductive charm draws attention to the vital role he plays in the novel as well as on the stage. It is likely that Colette chose his name because of its association with Marcel Proust, the novelist of sexual codes par excellence in France in the 1920s. The two remarkable authors had met and knew each other's work. Other parts of this book point out similar probable references to Proust not only in Colette's choice of characters' names but also in their traits (in *Chéri*, for example, in Chapter 1) and in the linguistic terms used to describe them, as in the analysis of "fée" in the following text.

In my reading, entitling the chapter "A la Mode de Paris" in English best conveys the appetite for the handsome actor who dominates the episode, given that we use "à la mode" in the United States for an ice cream topping and to signify considerable style, which Marcel possesses. Enid McLeod and Una Vincenzo Troubridge use the title "The Rage of Paris," choosing a colloquial expression, "rage," that appropriately connotes the homophobia of the angry chatelain who stops the embroidering sessions, though the term has become rarer in English. Andrew Brown chooses the innocuous, less insightful "Paris Fashions."

One example stands out among others in distinguishing among the various translations of this chapter's vocabulary of same-gender relationships: the word "fée." This occurs when the innkeeper, in gossiping with the young notary's wife, states "Une vraie fée!," "a real fairy," in reference to Marcel, the creator of a finely embroidered piano cloth.[13] Was the word "fée" used for gay men in 1923? What is arguably the best French/French dictionary covering that time period, the *Trésor de la langue française* does not include this usage.[14] The *Oxford English Dictionary*, however, does derive the usage of the word "fairy" from the Old French "faerie," "faierie," "feerie," "fae," and "fay."[15] The expression "mains [...]" or "doigts de fée" ("hands [...]" or "fingers of a fairy") often used to refer to a woman who sews well—and this appears in Proust[16]—corroborates the conclusion that "fée" could have referred to a gay man. In other words, in using the term "une vraie fée," the innkeeper may be identifying him as a gay person through the word's frequently pejorative connotation in a homophobic culture.

With this example, Colette writes a new tongue to go beyond sexuality understood as a pathology, that is, creates an innovative language that not only censures same-gender relationships and incest but also has the flexibility to transcend those prohibitions. Here she reveals a fascinating instance of how the linguistic resources of French in the 1920s both enabled and limited Colette's writing. In translating "une vraie fée" as "a real fairy with a magic wand," my attempt is to graft the latent bisexual voice (which enables) onto the everyday censorial language (which limits) as does the hybrid original.

The earlier translators have omitted the word, probably because of its negative connotation. They have used "like an angel,"[17] which, while referring to a being who is sometimes female, seems inappropriate for behavior not usually described as angelic, or "he's so talented,"[18] in which the idea of talent is genderless:

> Je verse le lait chaud de M. D'Avricourt et j'inscris la commande [...] Oui, madame, il loge ici [...] Ah! madame, on ne dirait jamais un comédien! Une voix comme une jeune fille [...] Et sitôt sa promenade faite après le déjeuner, il rentre dans sa chambre et il prend son ouvrage.

—Son ouvrage?
—Il brode, madame! Une vraie fée! Il finit un dessus de piano au passé, on l'exposerait! Ma fille a relevé le dessin.[19]

Given the centrality of bisexuality in the novel as a whole as I have been reading it, and the humorous, affectionate caricature of the gay actor here, despite the pejorative connotation, a better translation would be:

> I'll pour Monsieur d'Avricourt's hot milk and I'll write up the order [...] Yes, madame, he's staying here [...] Oh, madame, you'd never think he was an actor! He has the voice of a young girl [...] And as soon as his walk is over after lunch, he goes back to his room and takes up his work." "His work?" "He does embroidery, madame! He's a real fairy with a magic wand! He finished a piano cloth in satin stitch that you could put on display! My daughter copied the design.

Marcel's skillful handling of a sword as if it were a riding whip, along with an imaginary sheath for the sword, his antelope- or gazelle-like eyes and their thick lashes, and especially his embroidering and female voice are examples of a language that is predominantly pejorative in its non-literary usage to describe a gay man.[20] Colette gives such words a new form by incorporating them in her autobiographical novel whose underlying coherence considered synchronically transforms its homophobic connotations into desirable ones. Her new language links the gay man to the mother and thus conveys the author's unconscious desire.

French and English are similar in referring to the deer family to evoke a woman's beauty, especially her eyes, another part conveying the narrator's and author's longings for the same sex. One often hears "Bambi" used as an adjective to describe thick eyelashes. English frequently employs "doe" to speak of the large, soft, dark shape of a woman's eyes. The translators use the literal "gazelle" or "antelope." These choices are rare in current English usage, compared to their counterparts in French: "la châtelaine félicita publiquement, après le spectacle, M. Marcel d'Avricourt, grand premier rôle, un long jeune homme agréable, qui maniait l'épée comme une badine et voilait, sous des cils touffus, de beaux yeux d'antilope."[21] For this reason, the more frequent "doe" eyes are appropriate here: "the chatelaine congratulated M. Marcel d'Avricourt, the principal player, tall, friendly, and young, who handled his sword as beautifully as if it were a riding whip and whose lovely doe eyes were veiled by thick lashes." Beyond her mention of his abundant, long lashes, the narrator refers to Marcel's eyes in the passage on his discretion in averting his gaze while distributing holy water to blushing young women as he aids in the ceremony of Sunday mass.[22]

Colette's focus on the gaze, along with her insights on sexuality, both homosexual and heterosexual, demonstrates her prescience. Her writing is among the earliest to document the increasing significance of the use of the eyes in sexual orientation. Jean-Paul Sartre and Simone de Beauvoir will write about the gaze, for example, in the 1940s and 1950s. The look has also become a central idea in literary and film studies on sexuality/gender, especially in Laura Mulvey's theory of the "male gaze."[23] It is therefore not surprising that Colette was among the first to write on film though as far as I know she does not talk about the significance of the look in discussing the new art form. While the topic of the gaze does not appear much to my knowledge in criticism on the author, or translation and gay studies, it is probable that Colette is expressing a preference here for averting one's eyes as a mode of homosexual seduction over using them as a heterosexual form of appropriation. According to Mulvey's theory, the latter is often male, with both character and spectator/reader taking possession of the female while she watches him and/or them looking at her.

The translations miss other opportunities to recreate the erotic play of the eyes. The young notary's wife, the narrator tells us, "n'avait pas froid aux yeux," literally "did not have cold eyes."[24] Troubridge and McLeod write "was by no means shy"; Brown chooses "was no wallflower."[25] Colette's mention of the eyes here in describing the wife is significant because of its context. Right before this description, the narrator mentions Marcel's veil of thick lashes and his averted gaze as part of the gay man's seductive behavior attracting not only men but the woman in question and the other females discussed in the following text. "The young notary's wife had a coquette's eye for handsome men" is for this reason a better translation.

Additional significant instances of the need for the translation to retain the references to the gaze include the early description of Marcel mentioned above, where he is distributing holy water to the girls in a town called "Saint-Sauveur," ("Holy-Savior," an ironic name for the village as I will explain). "[He] withdrew without so much as a glance at their emotion," which I retain, recreates the discrete, seductive, averted gaze while Brown's translation does not: "He strode off without paying the least attention to their excitement."[26] Colette's anticlericalism and implied critique of the monotheism shaping normative heterosexuality emerges in the irony here in the town's Christian name and elsewhere in the novel, for instance, in the chapter "The Curate on the Wall." There the narrator mistakes the word "presbytère" for the hermaphroditic snail. In this way, Colette brings together the themes of Catholicism and non-normative sexuality more than once in the novel.

Catholic ritual, representative of the monotheism shaping sexuality in the West, including its stimulation of the senses, both conveys irony and adds intensity via the erotic play of the eyes in a final example. When Marcel is caught "in flagrante delicto"—the chatelain returns to find the men of the village embroidering and the women emitting sighs, which offer "incense and praise" to the "high priest" arousing their transport—Colette again points out that his gaze is not directed at females: "son regard oriental ne s'abaissait point sur elles"[27] once more uses the averted gaze as discrete and seductive behavior. The translators have chosen a version that is at odds with an appealing Marcel who is not arrogant: "his oriental gaze did not deign to lower itself to them;" "upon whom his Oriental eyes disdained to rest."[28] I translate, "His oriental gaze did not look down at them," avoiding disdain and keeping the problematic "oriental" to describe the doe eyes since it is most in keeping with the equally troubling French and proper in a sense to describe the beautiful almond shape.

While "Mode de Paris" ("The Rage of Paris") is the strongest evidence for the bisexual subtext, the desire for the mother and its implications for translating the text emerge early in the novel, for instance, in the chapter "Jalousie," strategically inserted right after Chapter 1 expressing her guilt.[29] The title reveals, beyond the father's resentment of his wife's flirtation with the local shopkeepers, the narrator/daughter's own version of this fundamental human emotion. She loves her mother and resents the latter's concern for her husband. The French makes clear that the chapter plays a critical role in unconsciously voicing the narrator's desire for her mother, in fact, sparked by the parents' continuing passion for each other that is its ostensible content. The daughter, awaiting the return of her mother from her trip to the butcher's to procure the shoulder of lamb for the evening meal, is astonished at the intensity of her feelings of happiness when she hears her mother's elegant footstep, sees her turn the street corner and walk down toward her. The narrator's astonishment, coupled with resentment, continues when the mother asks about her husband's whereabouts. The daughter wants her mother to inquire after *her*, not her father.

Other elements in the chapter serve to convey the narrator's desire by linking the two women: she points out that she herself is fifteen, an adolescent, often said to be prone to blushing like the mother who, though fifty-four, blushes when engaging with her jealous husband. These memories connote sexuality in no uncertain terms: the skin reddening from embarrassment (mentioned more than once), the mother's breasts pushed up by her corset, and especially the description of the daughter's appetite and repugnance for the meat products of the butcher, which mirror her complex feelings for her mother in this chapter and throughout the text. The narrator herself refers to her hiding the complicated response to the meat.[30]

In another example, "Coquette pour elle" ("coquette for her"), the daughter replaces the mother as a seductive woman. The words also imply that the daughter is seducing the mother. My version more directly and strongly signals the sexual meaning. The other translations, "in my vanity on her behalf" or "feeling vain on her behalf" do not.[31] They call attention primarily to the concern for appearance—the narrator had advised her mother to remove her unflattering apron before going to the butcher's.

In cases like this, my choice of words is completely different from the earlier ones. In others, for instance, in the holy water episode analyzed above, I have combined the best components of the earlier versions with my own to convey more clearly the narrator's desire. Colette's original title, for example, *La Maison de Claudine*, itself contributes to the fundamental misunderstanding of bisexuality and incest in the text, along with her use of the word "instinct." Given the fact that there is no Claudine in the narrative and that desire for the mother lies at the heart of the narrative, I follow McLeod and Troubridge in choosing the more appropriate title, *My Mother's House.* According to Maurice Delcroix, editor of the Pléiade original, Colette's publisher—and I would add, probably the author herself and her first husband, Willy, in financial need—wished to capitalize on the success of her Claudine series in the title choice.[32]

Another instance of my at times selective use of earlier versions appears in "Jalousie": "pricking the full bladders of pork or veal with a pin, then stomping them with her foot 'to make a water spout'" retains Troubridge and McLeod's "pricking," which appropriately connects the sexual image to its counterpart in "La Couseuse" ("The Sempstress").[33]

References to the voice, swords, as well as pins and needles in *La Maison de Claudine*'s language of sexuality produce an overlapping of Marcel, the mother, and the daughter. Colette implicitly associates the mother's voice, for instance, with that of Bel-Gazou who hears and recreates an imaginary song in the hazelnut in the final chapter. In the resonating and sensual conclusion of the novel, the narrator regrets both voices, now long gone.

Marcel's voice, too, bizarre and uncomfortable when one praises his embroidery and often characterized by crystalline laughter and sharp clucking sounds, comes to be connected to that of the child and mother, whose laugh is youthful, via the words "like a young girl." Colette writes: "comme une jeune fille [...]. fit deux ou trois petits cris bizarres et jeta quelques mots embarrassés [...]. [pousse], parmi les éclats cristallins de son rire, de petits gloussements aigus."[34] Like the mother, Marcel too is an object of desire for the narrator who longs for both a person of the same sex as well as a gay person of different sex. Associated, like both mother and daughter, with a sword-like needle, he is an obvious signifier of homosexuality. Given the needle's association with masculinity as well as with femininity, as further explained below, he is a critical part of the repressed bisexual subtext within the underlying coherence of the novel.

The ending clearly celebrates the child in the woman in a nonreductive way as does Philippe Sollers in his *Portrait de femmes* and helps to explain why so many readers see Colette's novel primarily as idealized memories.[35] One of the many questions posed by this intriguing narrative, however, is more problematic. How to cultivate a child's perspective without infantilizing others, or oneself, since the novel focuses on the young girl's incestuous love for her mother? In other words, is it possible to keep one's earlier creative self in a prohibited relationship for one's own pleasure and psychological need without damage? In Colette's case, the question is particularly relevant in her later critical relationship with her abusive first husband, Willy, as I discuss throughout this book.

An examination of translations of the chapter entitled "La Couseuse" ("The Sempstress") gives further examples demonstrating the need for this updated version of the novel and the problems it raises. Here the narrator describes her misgivings about teaching her daughter to sew. While sewing is a defining activity for the beloved Sido and the attractive Marcel, implicitly conveying sexual activity and appeal in the novel overall, it is more problematic in the daughter. One can well imagine that the narrator, given her awareness of the dangers implicit in bourgeois notions of femininity, might well be wary of encouraging Bel-Gazou to sew. The narrator states, however, that she has misgivings not because of the stereotype that a girl must sew but because her daughter is silent and can think while sewing—behavior otherwise highly prized in Colette. Here, the daughter reflects and questions when a man might put his arm around a woman. Her mother must admit that "it depends":

> Mal nouveau? Fléau que je n'avais point prévu? Assise dans une combe d'herbe, ou à demi enterrée dans le sable chaud et le regard perdu sur la mer, je sais bien qu'elle pense. Elle pense "à gros bouillons" lorsqu'elle écoute, avec une fausse discrétion bien apprise, des répliques jetées imprudemment en pont par-dessus sa tête. Mais il semble qu'avec le jeu de l'aiguille elle ait justement découvert le moyen de descendre, point à point, piqûre à piqûre, un chemin de risques et de tentations. Silence [...] Le bras armé du dard d'acier va et vient [...] Rien n'arrête la petite exploratrice effrénée. À quel moment faut-il que je lance le "hep!" qui coupe brutalement l'élan?[36]

Andrew Brown's "She thinks with effervescent speed when she is listening" for "Elle pense 'à gros bouillons,' lorsqu'elle écoute" adequately renders Bel-Gazou's vitality and intelligence, especially considering her name, which carries the association with sparkling water ("gazeuse") along with human and bird language.[37] "Her thoughts normally gush forth with effervescent speed while she listens" would retain the best part of Brown's rendering and more effectively use the image of a spurting liquid to convey the sexuality developing in the serious young thinker as well as the more rapid pace of her thinking.

The translators, however, have missed an opportunity to render a sexual connotation that is present in the passage and more in keeping with the novel's subtext as a whole: "stitch by stitch, prick by prick" for "point à point, piqûre à piqûre." McLeod and Troubridge as well as Brown choose "stitch by stitch, point by point."[38] In addition, retaining "I" as the subject of the third sentence here, as does Brown but not McLeod and Troubridge, conveys better the identification of the narrator with her daughter, which Colette enacts in the original:

> Is this a new evil? A plague that I had never anticipated? I know very well that she's thinking, seated on a patch of grass or half-buried in the hot sand, the gaze far away, looking at the sea. Her thoughts normally gush forth with effervescent speed while she listens to remarks as they are carelessly tossed off above her head, with a feigned discretion she has learned. But it seems that with the play of the needle, she has in fact discovered a way to progress down the path of danger and temptation, stitch by stitch, prick by prick. Silence. The arm bearing the dart comes and goes [...] Nothing stops the frenetic little explorer. When shall I shout "Stop!" and cut off the flow of energy with one blow?

Colette suggests here that sewing, like maternal authority and sexuality, can take various forms. She includes an ironic reference to the clever Philomène de Watteville, from the work of an author on whom she has written well, Honoré de Balzac. In his novel, *Albert Savarus*, Watteville destroys the brilliant career of her unfaithful lover by revealing his treachery using objects normally connoting the feminine, that is, the needle and embroidery.

It is also ironic but not surprising that the male images of "the prick" and "the sword" convey lesbian desire here as they often do. The choice of these images enables Colette to add complexity to the representation of same-gender attraction and especially to stand for bisexuality by combining "male" and "female" icons. The latter include "the thimble" and "the home" in the novel's title. The needle illustrates the combination of male and female icons particularly well: male because sword- and phallus-like as well as female because of its link to sewing.

In the same chapter on Bel-Gazou lies the passage in which Colette comes closest to revealing the conviction that all of us are bisexual. In reflecting on her daughter's increasing sexual awareness in the chapter's moving conclusion, the narrator refers to "l'instinct le plus majestueux et le plus trouble"; "that most majestic and most disturbing of instincts" in Troubridge and McLeod; "that most majestic and murky of all instincts" in Brown.[39] In Colette's novel, social forces and political issues are at stake at least as much if not more than biology in the depiction of sexuality, especially of homosexuality. I am thinking, for example, of the fact that it is the most powerful male authority in the town, representative of patriarchal culture, the chateau owner, who banishes the actors in "The Rage of Paris." In this context, "pulsion" and "drive" are words in French and English, respectively, that are more precise than her choice of "instinct." The meaning of the latter word, kept in both translations, is biological in the two languages. Laplanche and Pontalis point out the greater precision of "pulsion" and "drive" in their discussion of French and English translations of Freud's German "trieb" in their entry on "instinct/drive."[40] The effort to translate Colette more adequately into English leads to the unexpected discovery that, in the novel's context, she herself may have chosen the less appropriate word to convey "that most majestic and disturbing of drives," at least with the hindsight provided by *The Language of Psychoanalysis.*

Colette is thus a social and political historian to the degree that she depicts the transformations in women's sexuality and the parent–child relation underlying it in the early part of the twentieth century. She embodies a complex bisexual code in *La Maison de Claudine.* Keywords especially in such chapters as "Jalousie" ("Jealousy"), "Mode de Paris" ("The Rage of Paris"), and "La Couseuse" ("The Sempstress") including "fée" (fairy), "coquette," and "instinct" (drive) are part of a hidden language, which my new translation takes pains to render. Writing Colette in English is an ethical as well as an aesthetic enterprise given that contemporary societies often continue to label this language perverse. The close reading of *La Maison de Claudine* incorporated in the new translation establishes that a bisexual subtext is at play extensively and fundamentally in the folds of her novel including both a linear narrative of a young girl approaching adulthood in heteronormative society and the pervasive incestuous longing for a loving, creative mother.

Notes

1 Julia Kristeva, *Female Genius,* v. 3, *Colette,* trans. Jane Marie Todd (New York, Columbia University Press, 2004),. https://literarygitane.wordpress.com/2020/11/01/la-maison-de-claudine/.

2 Doris Lessing, Foreword to *Claudine's House,* trans. Andrew Brown (London: Hesperus Press: 2005), p. vii.

3 Colette, "La Maison de Claudine," in *Œuvres,* vol. II, ed. Claude Pichois et al. (Paris: Gallimard, 1986), pp. 965–1084.

4 See "The Thimble and the Needle: Translating *La Maison de Claudine*," *Palimpsestes*, vol. 24 (2012): 131–147; see also "Translating Colette: Bisexuality and Modernism in *La Maison de Claudine*." In *Translation and Literary Studies: Homage to Marilyn Gaddis Rose*, eds. Marella Feltrin-Morris, Deborah Folaron, and Maria Costanza Guzman (New York: Routledge, 2016), pp. 16–24.

5 Colette, "*My Mother's House*," in *My Mother's House and Sido*, trans. Una Vicenzo [sic] Troubridge and Enid McLeod (New York: Farrar, Straus and Giroux LLC, 1981), pp. 1–141; Colette, *Claudine's House*, trans. Andrew Brown (London: Hesperus, 2006), pp. 1–164.

6 Colette, *My Mother's House*, trans. Troubridge and McLeod. See also Pierre Schneider, "Paris: Fresh Look at Colette's Work," *The New York Times* (April 9, 1973). https://archive.nytimes.com/www.nytimes.com/books/99/10/17/specials/colette-fresh.html.

7 Julia Kristeva, "Ni Dépression ni perversion: éclosion," in *l'Herne Colette*, ed. Gérard Bonal et Frédéric Maget (Paris: L'Herne, 2011), pp. 19–28; this essay also appears as "Ni Dépression ni perversion: l'éclosion Colette" in her *Pulsions du temps* (Paris: Fayard, 2013), pp. 305–328.

8 Carol Mastrangelo Bové, *Language and Politics in Julia Kristeva: Literature, Art, Therapy* (New York: SUNY Press, 2006), p. 63.

9 Simone de Beauvoir, "The Married Woman," in her *The Second Sex*, trans. Constance Borde and Sheila Malovany-Chevallier (New York: Vintage, 2011), p. 445.

10 Colette, *La Maison de Claudine*, p. 1082.

11 Kristeva, *Colette*, 168–172.

12 Colette, *La Maison de Claudine*, p. 968.

13 Colette, *La Maison de Claudine*, p. 1022.

14 *Trésor de la langue française: Dictionnaire de la langue du XIXe et du XXe siècle (1789–1960).* http://www.atilf.fr/tlfi.

15 *Oxford English Dictionary*, s.v. "fairy (n.), sense 4.c," December 2023, https://doi.org/10.1093/OED/278102892.

16 Marcel Proust, "*Le Côté de Guermantes*," in *À la recherche du temps perdu*, vol. II, ed. Pierre Clarac & André Ferre (Paris: Gallimard, 1954), p. 215.

17 Colette, *My Mother's House*, p. 82

18 Colette, *Claudine's House*, p. 76.

19 Colette, *La Maison de Claudine*, p. 1022.

20 Colette, *La Maison de Claudine*, pp. 1022–1023.

21 Colette, *La Maison de Claudine*, p. 1022.

22 Colette, *La Maison de Claudine*, p. 1023.

23 Laura Mulvey, "Visual Pleasure and Narrative Cinema," *Screen*, vol. 16, no. 3 (Autumn 1975): 6–18.

24 Colette, *La Maison de Claudine*, p. 1022.

25 Colette, *My Mother's House*, p. 81; Colette, *Claudine's House*, p. 76.

26 Colette, *My Mother's House*, p. 81; Colette, *Claudine's House*, p. 76.

27 Colette, *La Maison de Claudine*, p. 1023.

28 Colette, *Claudine's House*, p. 78; Colette, *My Mother's House*, p. 83.

29 Colette, *La Maison de Claudine*, pp. 974–978.

30 Colette, *La Maison de Claudine*, p. 975.

31 Colette, *My Mother's House*, p. 16; Colette, *Claudine's House*, p. 14.

32 Colette, *La Maison de Claudine*, p. 1607.

33 Colette, *My Mother's House*, p. 16.
34 Colette, *La Maison de Claudine*, pp. 1022–1023.
35 Philippe Sollers, *Portrait de femmes* (Paris: Gallimard, 2013), p. 69. The recent death of and commentary on Sollers called my attention to the subtle insight into women's psychology in his novels, which are little known in the United States.
36 Colette, *La Maison de Claudine*, p. 1081.
37 Colette, *Claudine's House*, p. 155.
38 Colette, *My Mother's House*, p. 137; Colette, *Claudine's House*, p. 155.
39 Colette, *La Maison de Claudine*, p. 1082; Colette, *My Mother's House*, p. 138; Colette, *Claudine's House*, p. 157.
40 Jean Laplanche and Jean-Bertrand Pontalis, *The Language of Psycho-analysis*, trans. Donald Nicholson-Smith (New York, Norton, 1973), p. 216n.

Chapter 3

GIGI: THE IMPORTANCE OF THE UNCLE

More than twenty years after publishing *Chéri*, Colette continued to explore in *Gigi* (1944),[1] the fundamental prohibition enabling the social contract, the incest taboo, and its ramifications for women's psychology in a changing world. Known for her critique of heterosexual love and marriage, she celebrates them here in a late anomalous novel and its romantic fantasy of an adolescent and an older father figure. *Gigi* in fact embeds Colette's exploration of the social contract and its prohibition in the narrative, enabling the reader to reflect on a young woman's decision to follow her desire. The author's foundational relationship with her first husband, Willy, is clearly one of the sources for the novel. While *Gigi* on its surface does not replay the events of Colette's life, I argue that it is an example of her invention of autofiction and thus of her contributions to modernism, as I will examine.

In the novel, fifteen-year-old Gigi raises questions about love with a womanizing thirty-three-year-old man in dialogue presented by a third-person limited narrator. The narrative's subtext has Colette setting out problems in and through a young woman's entanglement with the incest taboo. This donnée sets the dramatic stage for a deep exploration of social and gender conflicts waiting to be played out in a nineteenth-century jewel box of French corruption.

The novel's semblance of popular romance fiction misleads critics, biographers, and mainstream readers alike who conclude that, while entertaining, it is not worth serious attention. Jerry Aline Flieger, for instance, who has written the excellent analysis of Colette's autobiographical writing discussed in my preceding chapters and below in this one, does not mention the title.[2] The fine biographer of the author, Judith Thurman, says that she wrote it while sick and bed-ridden in Nazi-occupied Paris as if to excuse her for having written an anomalous weak narrative capitulating to fantasy. She calls the novel "a delicious bagatelle," mellow and nostalgic, with a fairy-tale ending. Earlier, in her introduction to Roger Senhouse and Patrick L. Fermor's translation of the novel, she writes: "*Gigi*—written in the bleakest months of World War II—is the best known [of her works] to English-speaking readers, somewhat unfortunately, if only because its promise of happiness so misrepresents Colette's view of love [Vincente Minnelli's film version is an important factor in making her known in the US]."[3]

While there are elements of popular romance fiction in the text, the novel deserves the serious attention lacking in Flieger and Thurman, in fact, because of the way *Gigi* incorporates them, as I will explain. This chapter, informed by Julia Kristeva's *Colette*, provides a psychoanalytic close reading of *Gigi* absent in her in-depth study to prove that the narrative incorporates but goes beyond the usual versions of that genre, especially in its exploration of incestuous/incestual desire.[4]

One could argue that in this chapter and indeed throughout my book, the methodology revealing what is lacking in other critics resembles the paranoid reading famously identified by Eve Sedgwick. She called for a reparative literary approach, which does not try to uncover hidden meanings ignored by earlier readers. I am doing so but also include reparative elements to the extent that Kristeva, Flieger, Engelking, and others inform my reading. My analysis also tries "to account for the very queer pleasures [paranoid readings] ostensibly seek to enable," as Ellis Hansen recommends in an article on Sedgwick.[5]

In brief, literary critics tend to ignore or minimize the social prohibition in reductive readings of *Gigi*, if they consider the novel at all. Reducing the tale to a simple and stereotypical adolescent romance, they are responding this way partly out of nostalgia for a precious youth, also present in the novel, as do many readers of the earlier book, *La Maison de Claudine* (see Chapter 2).[6]

In recent decades, however, critics and theatrical producers have come to see the troubling elements in an older man's intense interest in a young girl. Vincente Minnelli's film version, particularly its widespread use of Maurice Chevalier's song, "Thank Heaven for Little Girls," throughout the movie has made them aware of the potentially pedophilic message. I am thinking especially of his much remarked clichéd "Frenchness," its associations with sexuality, and that glint in his eye.

Tama L. Engelking, for example, documents this awareness in an article focused on the appeal of Colette's writing in adaptations for the stage and screen in French and English. As mentioned above, Minnelli's film, for example, is responsible at least in part, for bringing knowledge of Colette to English speakers. Having noted Chevalier's "Frenchness," Engelking goes on to speak of an edgy *Gigi* compelling attention and overlooked. She examines the Broadway production of 2015, stating, "By eliminating the naughty bits in an effort to cater to modern tastes, Thomas had essentially smoothed out the edginess that made Colette's original story so compelling, flattening

Gigi down to a 'regular' love story that avoided the exploitation factor of earlier versions."[7] Such critics, however, do not identify the incest taboo lurking in the film and the book on which it is based. Nor do they address the way in which Colette weaves elements of her life along with the critique of womanizing, heterosexuality, and marriage in a romantic fantasy via the character Gigi and in the narrative considered in its entirety. Among these woven threads, it is not primarily her life, the woman apart from her writing that is the subject of my interpretation here but rather her psyche as revealed in her novels, as explained in my Introduction. The two, however, exist in a complex relationship that is difficult to untangle, given that the author bases her fiction on episodes from her life. As Jerry Aline Flieger concludes in 1992, Colette's autobiographical "I" is paradoxical and difficult to pin down.[8] One of the novelist's principal contributions to modernist literature is in fact her invention of what Serge Doubrovsky in 1977 had called "autofiction" as I will explain.

Insightful critics of this novel, including Kristeva, note, for example, how Colette echoes her age difference from her first husband in the relationship between the sixteen-year-old Gigi and the thirty-three-year-old Gaston.[9] A similar gap exists in the fictive couple Léa/Chéri as well as in the author's relationship with her stepson Bertrand (see Chapter 1) and with her mother in *La Maison de Claudine. Colette* implies that the complex entanglement of lived experience including the problematic rapport with a "family" member of vastly different ages in her fiction forms the author's sense of identity as it develops over time. Kristeva writes, "The written flora and fauna thus become the true and only metamorphoses of jouissance and trace the metaphorical alphabet of ecstasy that brings her into being and confers her ultimate reality on her." She goes on to explain, as I understand this in the context of her book, that Colette engages in a prohibited relationship, inhuman or monstrous, particularly with her mother on an unconscious level, which she transforms by means of writing into the birth of her best and truest self.

> In an ingenious intuition, Colette guesses that it is by appropriating her mother, by creating the mythical figure of Sido, that she will be able definitively to transmute perversion—*père-version*, turning toward the father—into *mère-version*, turning toward the mother, to reconcile herself with her always somewhat humiliated femininity and to finally install herself in the oblatory sensuality of a henceforth fateful writing.[10]

Kristeva's reading corroborates the import of the most helpful psychoanalytic theory, criticism, and fiction. In other words, a useful approach to interpreting a novel is to probe the connections to the author's earlier writing as well as to her or his biography in an effort to decipher the underlying fears and desires in the quest for identity, in Colette's case, emotions and sensations that a forbidden love object arouses.

Serge Doubrovsky's theory and practice have also contributed to an understanding of the processes lying beneath and generating literary texts, for instance, in his analysis of Marcel Proust in *La Place de la madeleine*.[11] He has in fact coined the term "autofiction" to refer to the hybrid nature of Colette's writing—autobiography and fiction.

Here, I uncover both the ways in which Colette explores the incest taboo and how the exploration brings a prescient version of modernism to writing. Reading the novel carefully and in the context of her other writing, namely *Chéri* and *La Maison de Claudine*, leads to a more informed sense of the major literary movement. While appearing primarily to celebrate heterosexual love and marriage, the novel has the attentive reader reflect on the problem of incest as well as that of womanizing, both of which have continued to figure prominently in literature[12] and to plague contemporary societies throughout the world. The confrontation with the patriarchal social contract's clauses restricting one's physical and psychic life appears in the strongest modernist women writers contemporary with or following Colette as I and others have pointed out.[13]

A perusal of the first pages of the novel reveals Colette's portrayal of an adolescent romance and weaves into it a less visible tale of incestual, even incestuous desire, which my psychoanalytic reading uncovers. I place quotation marks around "child" because, while her calendar age makes her a teenager, her words and actions, including those of her family, portray a girl very much as a "child" while at the same time gifted with great intelligence and creative thinking. In Gigi, Colette creates a beautiful and precocious "child" of fifteen who, beginning with a strong affection for a father figure, develops a passionate love, in fact, an adolescent passion fraught with fear, for a man who is a well-known womanizer.

It is one of Colette's strengths as a novelist that she can reveal in a clear, convincing way multiple perspectives in her narrative, going beyond the primary focus on Gigi. The third-person text uses conversation and a limited narrator to include the words and thoughts of the thirty-three-year-old "uncle" Tonton, as well as of Grandmother Alvarez and Aunt Alicia. The reader understands from these various points of view how the "child" becomes the future love object whom these others have been grooming for her later role. On the surface of the text, Colette stages a Pygmalion-like plot depicting an adolescent romance leading to a happy end once Gigi's development results in the perfect mate for Gaston.

While telling a primarily happy story of adolescent romance via a variety of perspectives, especially that of the "child," Colette's text, however, goes beyond that in ways that call attention to the unnamable problems involved. Gigi's fear is one element of a subtext raising fundamental questions for the "happy" conclusion.

The first pages return with her protagonist's full name, Gilberte, to echo the characters and substantial thought of Colette's contemporary Proust, as she had in *La Maison de Claudine.* The two had met more than once and took an interest in each other's work. Like *The Remembrance of Things Past*, though with significant differences as I will explain, her novels enable reflection on sexual codes and incest via memory and a "child's" point of view. Furthermore, Proust associates his Gilberte with the narrator's use of her as an exchange object after his initial intense love.[14] Colette's Gilberte fears such exploitation in her future with Gaston.

The first pages also begin the grandmother's efforts to ensure that a resistant Gilberte adheres to rules of "decency" (p. 4). "Decorum" (4) mistranslates "la décence" in Senhouse/Fermor's translation. In this way, Colette implies early on that this story deals with issues one should not speak of, which go beyond decorous behavior for a young girl as she matures, the plain concern of Alvarez's command that Gigi keep her knees together and to one side. The grandmother uses the word "la décence," ("decency") which has a sexual connotation in the novel's context, and Gigi refers to her sexuality discretely and humorously by objecting to the annoying need to keep her "you-know-what" covered (5).

Notable also in the context is the ambiguous suggestion of the grandmother's relationship with Gaston's father: the French states that she knew him very well and, as if to show its dangerous consequences, that Alvarez will affirm this only once in a conversation. The translation suggests less ambiguity by using the word "intimately." In both the French and English versions, Colette's text signals the possibility of biological incest in the relationship between the young girl and older gigolo, that is, that they are biologically niece and uncle given Alvarez's close tie to Lachaille senior (5). The narrator introduces additional elements in Gigi's and Gaston's behavior and words, which engage the reader in deciphering the ambiguous and disturbing presence of the taboo.For example, in recounting to Uncle the thorough list of advice Grandmother and Aunt have imposed on her, Gigi mentions their warning against the dangerous fathers who pick up their daughters after school. Colette thus reveals once again the underlying taboo lurking here as in *Chéri* and *La Maison de Claudine.* At the same time, the reader has noticed Gaston's body language, and responses to his "niece" that convey both his physical and emotional enjoyment. For instance, his smile breaks through sad eyes, revealing his pleasure in being with Gigi, relief from the pain and boredom of his usual love life, and unconsciously establishing its connection to and contrast with her as they discuss it (16). While Gigi and Gaston do not express incestual/incestuous longing directly, their dialogue and behavior in these instances, and others that I analyze below in the words of the limited third-person narrator, connote such desire.

In this context, the next section of the novel focuses on Gaston's former mistress Liane's attempted suicide, and speculation on his affair with someone else as a technique of unconscious anticipation. Without explicit references, the narrator implies connections to the potentially incestuous relationship. These pages have the reader think about the question of what Gaston will do next, with an inquisitive Gigi raising that very inquiry, as well as if he and Liane are leaving Paris to get married, and finally, if he would no longer be interesting if he married (27, 32). It becomes clear that the narrative is preparing implicitly for the answer that he may marry Gigi, thus problematizing this imminent outcome in light of both his blatant womanizing and his status as an incestual/incestuous object. Her angry outburst once he confesses his love raises a legitimate, serious question and thus increases the reader's anxiety for the future. She is correct in her interpretation of the brutality of an affection that exposes her to the suffering that may well result from his leaving her one day (60). In context, Gaston's love is "wicked," "horrible," and "terrible" for another reason as well, as I have been arguing.

Colette's innovative modernist writing once again, as in *Chéri* (see Chapter 1), displays the culminating cadence of difficulties in the couple's troubled responses to their feelings, especially Gigi's fears. On one level, this changing scenario seems insignificant in the unfolding romance leading to a happy ending, but, on another level, the careful reader feels suspense considering the taboo and the young girl's reactions. Gigi rejects Gaston when she initially learns of his proposal via Alvarez and does so again when he returns to speak directly to her. He too wavers in his responses, covering his desire with the lie—and she understands this—that he is coming back to retrieve his straw hat. In the end, the young girl expresses her love and accepts his offer of marriage but with knowledge of the danger she faces in marrying him. Colette's indirect language in the text shows that the dangers go beyond his infidelities to include incestual/incestuous desires.

Gigi's mother Andrée, the minor actor and singer at the Opéra comique, is a part of that indirection. She plays a bigger role here than it seems in the novel as a whole, proving the nuances of the simple popular romance. Andrée is, Colette suggests, what many women, including herself and Gigi, could and/or do become: a person isolated and melancholy in the extreme, living only via work, which does not adequately pay and/or recognize her for her abilities. One recalls the author's insights into women's writing (cited above in my Introduction) from the very novel Doubrovsky cites in discussing her innovation in creating autofiction: "Why should I stop my hand from gliding over this paper to which for so many years I've confided what I know about myself, what I've tried to hide, what I've invented and what I've guessed? At no time has the catastrophe of love, in all its phases and consequences, formed a part of the true intimate life of a woman."[15]

While the idea that one finds a sense of self while writing and/or in the completed text is a cliché, Colette's words nevertheless convey the alienation she experienced outside of her writing and the vital place of love in it. It is not a stretch to see these words and the character Andrée as evidence of the autofiction that Serge Doubrovsky defines in 1977, though he requires that the author include their name in the novel itself. Colette does so in the novel he cites, *Break of Day*, as one of the first examples of the genre.

Danielle Deltel's "Le Mécano du souvenir: les doublets autobiographiques chez Colette" corroborates that Doubrovsky's theory of autofiction applies to Colette's autobiographical novels. Her essay shows that these novels reveal the author's identity more accurately than the events and experiences of her life outside of the texts. As I read Deltel and her discussion of Doubrovky's theory, autofiction is a narrative in which the author inserts herself in an imaginary world in a way that conveys the truest sense of her identity.[16]

Tama L. Engelking's "Reading the Romance with Colette in 'La Lune de pluie' " both cites Doubrovsky and convincingly analyzes the novelist's writing just prior to her composing *Gigi*. The article discusses how she creatively incorporates elements of popular art—a topic to which I return below—in ways that overlap fiction and autobiography.[17] While Engelking does not discuss *Gigi* here, it is clear from my discussion earlier of her insightful remarks on it and its sanitizing Broadway adaptation, that she knows Colette's work and its popular elements well. It is likely in this context, as well as that provided by Kristeva and Deltel, that the author bases the character of Andrée at least in part on her own experience of isolation and melancholy in her relationships and writing, including her career.

The details in the text corroborate my sense of the significance of the mother's role. Grandmother Alvarez tells us that Andrée rejected a mill owner's proposal of marriage to be with a music teacher who left her in the end. The novel embeds this information in the response to Andrée's pejorative comment that Gigi is not very mature and will wind up a clothing model or salesperson, leading the reader to compare the actor and her daughter. The text presents Andrée as someone who, defeated in both her personal and professional lives, does not see clearly, and "sees everything in black" ("C'est ta solitude [...] qui te fait voir tout en noir") as Alvarez puts it, in her view because she is without a partner (22). She is able to fulfill her duties as a minor singer at the Opéra Comique and to communicate calmly with her mother. Though she does not suffer from the inability to speak rationally which is one of its worst symptoms, Andrée fits the definition of abjection in Kristeva's terms. Her speech lacks the vitality and desire that constitute the best version of the semiotic resources of language, except in her singing, which I discuss below.

The presence of Andrée as the sad mother figure further problematizes the daughter's decision to marry Gaston in the conclusion, not only in connection with his womanizing but also with his status as a paternal figure. Could Gigi be following in her mother's footsteps in marrying a man known for his abandonment of the women in his life, in fact, like her "father" in many ways, including the biological one?

Luckily for Gigi, Grandmother Alvarez is the loving authority figure, enabling her to develop a healthy relationship with herself and others. While Kristeva does not analyze the grandmother and mother in the context of Gigi's rapport with maternal figures, these characters along with Aunt Alicia are central in my psychoanalytic reading of the novel. Noteworthy in this regard are Gigi's comments seeking knowledge from and expressing affection for Alvarez against the backdrop of her home and biological mother. Speculating with some anxiety about Gaston's behavior after separating from his latest fling, Liane, the young girl embraces her grandmother and seeks assurances that she can remain in her home and not go to live with her aunt. Once Tonton has spoken to Alvarez about marrying her, she asks about her mother's absence at lunch and if Andrée in fact did not want to dine with them. In other words, Gigi is preoccupied with understanding her relationships with three maternal figures in her life: aunt, mother, and especially grandmother. In embracing Alvarez, Gigi indicates that she solidifies her links to her at the same time as her love for Gaston develops and she needs to reach a decision (34).

Flieger's theories on and criticism of Colette are relevant here. Without discussing *Gigi*, she calls attention to the importance of a woman's relationship with her mother in the pre-Oedipal phase.[18] In the best-case scenario of this stage in psychosocial development, the maternal figure is both a love object and an authority figure. Alvarez is such a mother for Gigi in the episode described above in which she embraces her principal caregiver after asking her questions about Gaston, Andrée's absence from lunch, and whether she can remain in her grandmother's home. The textual evidence supports the fact that the young girl's interaction with Alvarez has nurtured a strong psyche ready to make a difficult decision to marry the man she loves despite the fear that he may one day leave her.

Kristeva's detailed study of the novelist enables the reader both to connect this anomalous narrative to, as well as to distinguish it, from her earlier works. *Colette* calls attention to the difficulty critics have in understanding and classifying it in the context of the author's oeuvre. Kristeva discusses the overall strength of her portraits of French women, comparing them to those of Balzac, whose work the author of *Gigi* knew well and on which she had published. *Colette* shows that his talent and hers lie in creating the perfect image to convey his protagonists' "monstrous" sensuality, though it does not discuss the anomalous *Gigi* in connection with this topic.[19] Colette's character in the late novel does not fit the description of her typical female protagonists. According to Kristeva, and I agree, the novel affectionately presents a young woman who is both chaste and mature—a subject to which I return below.

She places the author of *Gigi* in Balzac's wake here, while also pointing out the anomaly of the novel's protagonist. Among her many insights into Colette in the context of Balzac, Kristeva states not only that the brilliant author of *The Human Comedy* demonstrated in his novels the central role of women and their "monstrous sensuality," but also that they play an important role in the rise of the bourgeoisie. She implies the same for the author of *Gigi* despite the late novel's anomaly.

Furthermore, the earlier chapter of Kristeva's book deals with the popular elements in it. Despite the anomaly of its protagonist, *Gigi* corroborates the idea that Colette's fiction, like that of Balzac, reveals the ways in which women's psychology shapes the rise of the middle class, including its aspirations and forms of writing, especially the invention of the novel. Kristeva explains how the tale of the young girl in training as a courtesan derives from vaudeville, a medium in which Colette famously performed. One recalls the scandal created by the breast she revealed on stage in such a performance.

Though Kristeva does not discuss in detail Balzac's fictional demonstration of the significant function of "the feminine" in the development of the middle class and the novel, her complex analysis of Colette's *Gigi* and its vaudevillian elements suggests the ways in which this book contributes to the ascension of middle-class art. In laying out these elements, *Colette* underlines the sociological naturalism in the depiction of Grandmother Alvarez and Aunt Alicia, the two cocottes. The melodrama and platitudes in the novel also derive from vaudevillian performance. In other words, the lack of serious reflection one associates with vaudeville (the plethora of references to control by the body, emotions, and clichés) can nonetheless become elements in skillful writing. These are characteristics that Colette incorporates and goes beyond, according to Kristeva. She concludes that these are not evidence of the novel's weakness. As I read her assessment, they instead contribute to its excellence as popular *and* high art, or popular art as serious as high art.

From her perspective, Colette's genius here resides especially in her amazing protagonist whose unconscious performs what is required to follow and satisfy her desire for Gaston. The portrayal of Gaston also excels in its understated revelation of a powerful love.

Further examples of the novel as a valuable form of popular fiction exist in the rich mixture and confusion of social classes in the behavior and speech of the courtesans, Grandmother Alvarez and Aunt Alicia, whose aspirations to wealth and respectability survive their engagement in sex work. The best example, however, is Gigi herself who somehow transcends her youth, family, and their limitations by intelligently asking all the right questions about their mixed lifestyle and identity. In response to Aunt Alicia's comment about "ordinary people," for example, she asks if she and her family are not such individuals themselves (37). In other words, she is the perfect example of a heroine of popular literature understood in the best sense and enabling a consideration of serious questions. Gigi miraculously and unconsciously achieves happiness, at least for a time, both within and outside of the social contract and without the author's providing explicit psychological analysis.

In the end, Kristeva—in clear disagreement with most other critics—gives high marks to *Gigi*, writing, "We are in the realm of the unsaid, and rarely has one of Colette's texts been so faithful to the primary calling of her writing, which is to show the *budding* of a passion and of a style rather than its *unfolding*."[20] Thus, it is in this popular novel that Colette is at her best in conveying the birth of unconscious desire for another in her writing, understood in the context of her *oeuvre complète*. The novel reveals a young woman whose love for Gaston finds a way to obtain him without being manipulative or pure. She acts intuitively, that is, shaped by both biological and social/political forces, as the context enables the reader to understand. The novel itself makes clear her physical and emotional responses to her lover/"uncle," for example in her enthusiastic acceptance of his invitation to take her to tea at the Versailles *Réservoirs*. This immediate context also includes her awareness of the sociopolitical situation of her love for a man renowned for his womanizing in the demi-monde, as her grandmother and aunt have informed her along with the knowledge that marriage would be the best outcome for her, at least for a time.

Beyond the novel itself, Colette's other writing provides helpful context for understanding *Gigi* and her eponymous protagonist. To focus on the novels included in this volume, I would point out the complex depiction of love and its emergence in her characters from forces that are biological, social, and political. Such a portrayal appears in different forms in her depiction of Léa's love in *Chéri* as well as that of the daughter for her mother in *La Maison de Claudine*. In other words, Colette's writing corroborates Kristeva's reading of

Gigi as acting intuitively upon the array of forces shaping her behavior in gaining Gaston's offer of marriage.

As in her comments on Balzac, Kristeva is insightful and thought-provoking in her discussion of Colette and Proust. According to her, while both ground their fiction in the child's experience, Colette's grounding is more innocent than Proust's. Kristeva uncovers more guilt and a greater sense of immorality in his writing as an incestuous replaying of the union with the mother. Colette's writing preserves the child's innocence to the degree that her tone is more positive in its celebration of the replay of incestual/incestuous love. This preservation helps to explain the joy in her conclusion to *Gigi*. While the novel's context highlights the problems raised by the marriage to the womanizer Gaston who may also be her step-uncle biologically, at the same time, it embraces those worrisome difficulties, for instance, via the protagonist's childlike simplicity in revealing her decision to her lover: "Alors…. Alors… Voilà. Bonjour… Bonjour, Gaston" ("So…So… There you are. How d'you do, Gaston, how d'you do?"[21] In this way, the happy ending reprises Colette's appreciation for the child's perspective as in the ending of *La Maison de Claudine* and affirms the possibility of a precious point of view that can survive in the adult.

The historical and material conditions of Colette's composing *Gigi* while Paris is under siege also inform my close reading of the text as a joyful embracing of a troubling event. Kristeva draws attention to the novelist's belief that writing/reading is the only remedy for the conflicts between nations. This late novel affirms that belief in its overall positive tone despite what Mark Giesser has recognized as its partial edginess and even darkness, which corroborates my reading of its complexities.[22]

Echoing the troubling question of escapism raised in *Chéri*, *Gigi* enables the reader to probe the happy ending as a form of escape from the real problems of womanizing and incest. Persisting in the affirmation of dealing with overwhelming difficulties, however, like the earlier novel, this one portrays a woman willing to confront rather than avoid.

Engelking's article on her novel *The Rainey Moon* discussed above provides more historical and material data in support of Colette's focus on engagement rather than escape. "Reading the Romance with Colette in 'La Lune de pluie'" discusses the escapist elements in the romance to show precisely that she engages seriously with that genre and the marginalized women who read such books.[23]

Both Engelking and Kristeva emphasize the strength of women writers and their contributions to social transformation rather than submission to or escape from the status quo. *Colette* refers to *Paris de ma fenêtre*, where the author of *Gigi* writing this novel during the Occupation speaks of the reading room as valuable to a solitary female. Colette alludes to Balzac's depiction of such a woman in his "A Man of Business." In other words, here, as Kristeva points out, Colette affirms her fierce love of books, especially fine novels like those included in *The Human Comedy*, in the context of both the war and her amorous relations.[24] It is also significant that the author of *Gigi* reprises Balzac's image of a woman alone with her book in the context of the instrumental role of females in the development of the novel as a middle-class invention, though Kristeva neither mentions this in her discussion of the image nor does she mention György Lukacs's and Ian Watt's works on the topic.[25] Implicit in her analysis of both the vaudevillian elements and of the roots of Colette's thinking during the German occupation, however, is the idea of fiction as a product of the bourgeoisie and especially of its women.

Thus, Colette leaves the reader with a murky ending, more complex than critics and editors recognize. In the scholarly Pléiade edition, Claude Pichois refers to the novel as "un conte bleu," (a fairy tale) but this comment itself suggests the complexity of the text given that it is embedded in a reference to Georges Bizet's *Carmen*, hardly a simple narrative.[26] It is not clear that Gigi has matured to the point of being aware of the consequences of her decision to marry Gaston. Is she unsure of what her future marriage will become and so decides to err on the side of potential happiness? It is also unclear if Gaston has decided he is no longer a parent figure/gigolo but is now a lover and friend to an adult Gigi. He too, however, will go forward, betting on making the right choice.

It is clear, however, that *Gigi* is more serious than popular, or popular in the best sense, with vital links to other major French authors such as Balzac and Proust. I have noted Colette's contributions to the modernist movement, especially the decidedly unconventional psyche of her female narrators and characters in their engagement with buried incestuous/incestual desire. This chapter and the preceding ones also call attention to the rhythmic cadences in the plot to convey the volatility and intensity of their emotions and sensations, particularly in the ending of *Gigi*, as well as of *Chéri*.

In conclusion, part of her innovative modernism also lies in her writing as autofiction. The intricate blending of biography and imagination in her novels forges a fragile sense of identity for her as Jorge Luis Borges recognizes in his own writing.[27] Stéphanie Michineau's insight into the special contributions of women to such autofiction corroborates Colette's innovations in modernist writing: she concludes her essay "L'Autofiction dans l'oeuvre de Colette" by referring to the genre as the privileged means of expression for women as a minority category at the beginning of the twentieth century in their struggle for agency and identity.[28] It is as if the stranger within emerges in her novels, establishing who she really is, that is, what she thinks, at least temporarily. While raising the specter of incestuous desire in a seeming fantasy, the novel *Gigi* attests to Colette's belief in avoiding cynicism and reductive thinking by taking a chance on a problematic love.

Notes

1 Colette, "*Gigi*," in *Oeuvres*, vol. IV, ed. Claude Pichois et al. (Paris: Gallimard, 2001/1944), pp. 433–476. Page numbers refer to the English translation of the novel in *Three Short Novels by Colette: Gigi, Julie de Carneilhan, Chance Acquaintances*, trans. Roger Senhouse and Patrick Leigh Fermor (New York: Farrar, Straus, and Giroux, 2001), pp. 1–68.

2 See Jerry Aline Flieger, *Colette and the Fantom Subject of Autobiography* (Ithaca: Cornell University Press, 1992).

3 See Colette, *Gigi, Julie de Carneilhan, Chance Acquaintances*, p. vii; see also her introduction to a new translation of Colette, *Chéri and the End of Chéri*, trans. Paul Eprile (New York: New York Review of Books Classics, 2022), Kindle, p. 7; and her review "Good, Clean Fun: A Revival of *Gigi*," *New York Review of Books* (April 7, 2015). https://www.newyorker.com/culture/cultural-comment/good-clean-fun-a-revival-of-gigi.

4 Julia Kristeva, "*Colette*," in *Female Genius*, vol. 3, trans. Jane Marie Todd (New York: Columbia University Press, 2004).

5 See Eve Kosovsky Sedgwick,"Paranoid Reading and Reparative Reading; or You're so Paranoid you Probably Think This Introduction is About you," in *Novel Gazing: Queer Readings in Fiction* (Durham, North Carolina: Duke University Press, 1997), pp. 1–37; see also Ellis Hansen, "The Future's Eve: Reparative Reading After Sedgwick," *South Atlantic Quarterly*, vol. 110, no. 1 (2011): 101–119. https://read.dukeupress.edu/books/book/636/chapter/128566/Paranoid-Reading-and-Reparative-Reading-or-You-re; https://read.dukeupress.edu/south-atlantic-quarterly/article-abstract/110/1/101/3506/The-Future-s-Eve-Reparative-Reading-after-Sedgwick?redirectedFrom=fulltext, respectively.

6 Another exception to the general misreading and/or neglect, which mentions the frequent reductive evaluation, is Susan Cohen's "An Onomastic Double Bind: Colette's *Gigi* and the Politics of Naming," *PMLA*, vol. 100, no. 5 (October 1985): 793–809.

7 See Tama L. Engelking, "Crossing Borders with Colette's *Gigi*," *The French Review*, vol. 93, no. 3 (2020): 102–115. https://works.bepress.com/tama_engelking/32/.

8 Flieger, p. 4.

9 Kristeva, pp. 271–272.

10 Kristeva, pp, 12–13.

11 *Writing and Fantasy in Proust: La Place de la Madeleine*, trans. Carol Mastrangelo Bové and Paul Bove (Lincoln and London: University of Nebraska Press, 1986).

12 Hortense Spillers speaks of the prevalence of the topic of incest in much literature, especially African American, in her *Black, White, and in Color: Essays on American Literature and Culture* (Chicago: Chicago University Press, 2003), p. 231.

13 See my *Language and Politics in Julia Kristeva: Literature, Art, Therapy* (Albany, NY: 2006), p. 5; see another discussion of this topic in Philippe Birgy and Aurélie Guillain's "Introduction," in "Modernism and the Obscene," *Miranda* 21 (2020). https://doi.org/10.4000/miranda.27682.

14 See my "Women and Society in Literature, or Reading Kriisteva and Proust," *After Theory, The Dalhousie Review*, vol. 64, no. 2 (1984): 260–269.
15 Colette, *Break of Day*, trans. Enid McLeod (New York: Farrar, Straus & Giroud, 1979), p. 62.
16 Stéphanie Michineau discusses Doubrovsky and Deltel in "L'Autofiction dans l'œuvre de Colette," *Semat: An International Journal*, vol. 1, no. 1 (2013): 1–9.
17 See Tama Engelking, "Reading the Romance with Colette in 'La Lune de pluie,'" *Modern Language Studies*, vol. 47, no.1 (summer 2017): 26–45; Doubrovsky makes his definition of autofiction more precise in 1999 when he explains in an interview that his term applies only to those texts in which the author gives their name to narrator and character. https://engagedscholarship.csuohio.edu/clmlang_facpub/142/.
18 Flieger, pp. 194–195.
19 Kristeva, p. 362.
20 Kristeva, p. 361.
21 Colette, "Gigi," in *Œuvres*, vol. IV, p. 476; Colette, *Gigi, Julie de Carneilhan, Chance Acquaintances*, p. 67, respectively.
22 See Mark Giesser's comments on his adaptation of *Gigi* in Nick Clark, "Gigi: How a west London theatre is putting the darkness back into a play best known as a sunny musical." *Independent* (October 17, 2015). https://www.independent.co.uk/arts-entertainment/theatre-dance/news/gigi-how-a-west-london-theatre-is-putting-the-darkness-back-into-a-play-best-known-as-a-sunny-musical-a6698421.html.
23 See Engelking, "Reading the Romance with Colette in 'La Lune de pluie'."
24 Kristeva, p. 368.
25 See György Lukács, *The Theory of the Novel*, trans. Anna Bostak (Cambridge, MA: MIT Press, 1974/1968); Ian Watt, *The Rise of the Novel* (Oakland, CA: University of California, 1957).
26 Colette, *Gigi* in *Oeuvres*, vol. IV, p. 1229, n.1.
27 See "Borges and I," in *Collected Fictions*, trans. Andrew Hurley (London: Penguin, 1999), p. 324.
28 *Semat* 1, no. 1: 1–9 (May 2013). https://www.naturalspublishing.com/files/published/96487z73y4td8l.pdf.

Chapter 4

MORE THAN A MUSICAL: MINNELLI'S *GIGI*

A close look at Vincente Minnelli's musical film *Gigi* (1958) uncovers ambiguities making it difficult to decide, especially today, if the movie is 1) celebrating incestuous/incestual desire or 2) enabling reflection on such a troubling phenomenon via the characters' attempts to cope with it, as in Colette's novel.[1] In this chapter, I examine this difficulty and consider how Minnelli's direction adapts Colette's vision.

His superb popular film introduced many Americans to Colette's name. Alan Jay Lerner's screenplay and lyrics, along with Frederick Loewe's music shape thought-provoking performances by Leslie Caron and Louis Jourdan with Maurice Chevalier adding dangerous charm. This version is upbeat, a Pygmalion operetta in which narrative, romance, and comedy resemble elements in Lerner and Loewe's Broadway musical, *My Fair Lady*, of two years before, but its engagement with the incest taboo makes it different and worth more attention than paid until now.

Seeming a less complex novel than Colette's others, *Gigi* in fact raises important and tough questions about an amorous relationship between "parent" and "child," as my preceding chapter shows. While psychoanalytic critics credit Julia Kristeva, along with other French feminists, with shifting the focus from a male-centered psychology to one more cognizant of the female, her theories and literary criticism in fact also bring new light to psychological formations in both sexes, as I will explain in this analysis of Minnelli's film and its unconscious subtext.

Focusing on the young Gigi and the father figure Gaston from Colette's novel, including its "happy" ending, the film also adds a character absent from it, Gaston's uncle, Honoré. He is Anita Loos's invention in her 1951 Broadway production based on the novel. Played by Chevalier, the addition has a significant impact on the movie's contradictory messages.

Minnelli uses Honoré to frame the narrative in a way that celebrates womanizing with emphasis on the love object before she matures. Such a beginning makes one uneasy over the suggestions of incestual relations.

The latter, as explained in my Introduction , engages individuals who play the role of child and parent without being related biologically. Biology does connect them in the more commonly used term "incestuous."

Chevalier introduces the story, addressing the viewer directly and calling attention to little girls as desirable because of their future growth into beautiful women. Gigi herself is among those photographed playing nearby with other youngsters in the Bois de Boulogne as the movie segues into the uncle's rendition of "Thank Heaven for Little Girls."

In this film, both Gilberte (her full name with the Proustian resonances discussed in Chapter 3) and Gaston, one could argue, confront and struggle to cope with a patriarchal hierarchy, which grooms a child to remain so in many ways. Following Colette's novel, Minnelli indirectly has the reader consider the conflicts posed by unequal power relations in the couple, which begins and persists as a version of a child–parent relationship. As in *Chéri*, incestuous desire, in the explicit form of a biologically related parent–child, never surfaces. There is, however, the possibility of such longings in the uncle–child relationship in both Colette's and Minnelli's *Gigi*.

Furthermore, Gigi's grandmother, Madame Alvarez, and Aunt Alicia try to educate her to conform eventually to the status of kept woman in the courtesan world of Paris, an infantilizing education in a sense. One could argue against this view that the position of a courtesan is like any other form of earning a living, as in the earlier novel, *Chéri*, in which it is a mother rather than a father figure who plays the role of parent. In my readings of both Colette and Minnelli, sex work, however, prevents development into mature human beings who should not have themselves treated as objects. Beyond the child/father relationship embedded in the text and which limits her agency, Gigi's education via Alvarez and Alicia would also thus infantilize her, though in a contradictory way, given that she would eventually be using an adult body to earn her living.

In a parallel plot, Honoré tries to educate Gaston in the ways of womanizing and succeeds but only in part. Before the final scene upending this success, Alvarez and Alicia collaborate to have Gigi accept the offer to become the mistress of the womanizer likely to leave her in the end, and she eventually does so.

Her acquiescence signals a worrisome turn in the young girl, who had been so resistant to life as a courtesan. In a scene following her well-argued, angry outburst when Gaston confesses that he loves her, she says only "I would rather be unhappy with you than unhappy without you." While this statement does convincingly reveal her love for him, it also shows that she sees only unhappiness in her future, having become inarticulate in considering her options as a young woman of intelligence and beauty. Her words also convey her fluctuating feelings given the earlier outburst: her longing to prevent ending up alone without the love of her life follows the powerful fear of abandonment by an unfaithful husband. Along with the song she sings soon after, mentioning that she is "too young to die," her brief statement shows a hint of abjection. Kristeva's theories on this psychic formation as one that can lead to difficulties in thinking and speaking clearly along with masochistic behavior supports this interpretation of Gigi's state at this point. The theory of abjection in *Powers of Horror* claims that human beings need the full resources of rational and sensual language to develop psychic well-being. While the former, the symbolic, relies on the relationship to a paternal figure, the latter, the semiotic, engages the child in attempts to reunite with a maternal one. The quest for this sensual language emerges from childbirth and infantile separation from the mother's body.[2]

The film portrays a young girl without the more usual presence of biological parents. The woman who gave birth to her, a minor singer in the Opera comique, is never on screen, only heard practicing arias. Her father never appears either. Thus, this context creates a need for Gigi to find proper replacements, that is Grandmother and Gaston.

The movie reveals how, in the painful quest for parental figures, she becomes less resolute than in scenes absent in Colette. In fact, she begins to behave like Gaston's earlier mistresses and reveals that Alvarez and Alicia have succeeded in their training. This behavior is masochistic in the context that convincingly portrays earlier her intense distaste for and resistance to such activity. A good example appears in Gigi's display of knowing how to choose the right cigar—that famous Freudian icon—for her man. In other words, Minnelli stresses that she becomes willing to adopt more conventional and troubling behavior in a way that Colette does not, though the young girl agrees to become a mistress in both the film and novel.

Minnelli's movie takes subdued notice of the couple's family histories, which, as in the novel, opens the possibility that Gigi's acquiescence would be incestuous as well as incestual. The presence of two womanizing father figures, "Uncle" Gaston and his own uncle, Honoré, on the one hand, enables the viewer to pick up more easily on the hidden taboo. That is, the presence of Chevalier's character makes visible the possible biological link between the two lovers as well as hinting at incestual and/or pedophilic desire in the repeated singing of "Thank Heaven for Little Girls" mentioned above. On the other hand, this doubling at the same time leads the viewer to accept the younger of the two men, Gaston, played by the dashing Louis Jourdan, as proper husband. This is especially the case in a conclusion satisfying in part the spectator's need to dispel the troubling possibility of an undesirable relationship, given his womanizing and the incestual/incestuous nature of their affair. That is, Gaston becomes the ethical lover and realizes that he should marry her, while Gigi is willing to become his mistress after resisting.

The film goes beyond the appearance and limitations of the more usual forms of popular culture as does Colette's vaudevillesque novel (see Chapter 3). In my view, this Hollywood musical, among the best, which won nine Oscars, compels the viewer to consider the possibility that one can overcome the impasses posed by incestual and possibly incestuous desire, but not without a struggle. The movie enables reflection on not only the explicit problem of womanizing but also the implicit one of incest, both of which continue to plague societies in many parts of the world.

The context of the film, namely the fact that Gigi's grandmother had a serious affair with Honoré and that Alvarez and Gaston are close, suggests that he could be her son, and therefore, Gigi's biological uncle. This shows that Gigi, profoundly attached to her father figure Gaston, is engaging in not only an incestual but also a potentially incestuous affair. While viewers of the film may not see the incest taboo at all in the movie, understanding it primarily as a celebration of joyful womanizing culminating in an even happier marriage, evidence from the film, including Honoré's and Alvarez's early affair, suggests otherwise. One could argue that this is unlikely given that Gaston's father appears in one scene and that Honoré mentions him in another. Even if Gigi's lover is not her biological uncle, the film makes clear that their relationship is that of "parent" and "child" and thus, that the young girl, profoundly attached to her father figure Gaston, engages in an incestual affair.

Minnelli's adaptation goes well beyond the novel on this point by adding to the evidence of Honoré's and Alvarez's relations in the past and thus of Gaston's being Alvarez's son. A scene both entertaining and fascinating due to its rhythm and timing, their duet "I Remember it Well," has the elderly couple remembering in vastly different ways their last and momentous encounter at the sea in Trouville, like a husband and wife married for a long time. Thus, the songs in the film do more than provide entertainment and convey significant content and context for understanding the characters and their relationships, namely that Gigi and Gaston's affair may well be incestuous as well as incestual.

In addition to the Trouville scene, the film's images and soundtrack, resources different from those of the novelist, convey the incest theme plainly in two references to spanking. In the first, the early carriage scene where he finds Gigi on the park bench having sung "I Don't Understand the Parisians!" (their obsession with sex), she asks him directly if he makes love all the time. Once he tells her to come along or he will spank her, she goes with him to the ice rink where he will see his current mistress, Liane. Later, in the movie's predominant setting, Gigi's small apartment, Gaston playfully hits her on the bottom. The behavior connotes both parental and sexual behaviors in a striking! visual image, especially in the context in which Minnelli presents it. That is to say, the first appears in a conversation about sex and the second in a familial setting.

The film episodically depicts family settings as scenes for erotic traffic incestuous in kind. Early examples take place in the "family home," with doting "father" Gaston giving caramels to Gigi, allowing his child to cheat in order to win during their playful card games, along with "mother" preparing cassoulet in the kitchen. "Mother" returns to the role of "grandmother" when "father" takes the family to the seashore at Trouville. When Honoré shows up, distracted from his pursuit of a young woman by "grandmother," and "I Remember it Well" ensues, we observe loving "grandparents" enjoying the sight of Gaston and Gigi playing on the beach with the donkeys in the oldest resort in Normandy, an image of familial values spanning many generations.

Other details reveal the combination of incestual/incestuous and romantic/sexual themes. Her beau Gaston expresses the desire for the maturing Gigi to return to wearing her youthful Scottish plaid frock (his words, "little Scots dress," suggesting a child's outfit). His rendition of the eponymous song repeats "She's a babe [...] a babe good for balancing on the knee." In addition, Gigi wants to return to having "father" Gaston give her caramels in the very scene in which she speaks of her resistance to getting into his bed knowing she would be leaving herself open to such behavior with other men once Gaston has tired of her.

A plethora of examples in fact conveys both Gigi's and Gaston's passion, which the context colors as the prohibited and repressed love between a child and her father. Displaying her keen interest in him, his unattached state, and his future, she poses questions about what he will do once Liane has abandoned him for a new lover. Her grandmother treats the inquiries like those of an annoying child, as in Colette's dialogue in the novel. Furthermore, Gaston serves her champagne behind her grandmother's back, suggesting his role as a disguised enabler of forbidden behavior.

The movie emphasizes that Gigi is a child: she is a young girl following in the footsteps of her "mother," Mamita, who, despite her being a courtesan, refused to continue her relations with the womanizer Honoré many years before. Also, the theme song "Thanks Heaven for Little Girls" plays throughout the soundtrack and returns in the ending with a chorus joining Honoré, as if many concur with his keen interest in women as children. Minnelli has him reappear as the commentator on the film who addresses the audience directly once again in the conclusion as in the opening.

There is no textual evidence in the movie to argue, against my reading of unconscious desire, that Gigi and/or Gaston know about and understand the risk involved in the incestuous love, strongly suggested to the viewer, for example, in the Trouville scene described above. A careful reading of the film helps decipher the young girl's limited awareness. Though she is unaware of his possible biological relationship to her, Gigi knows about Gaston's "love them and leave them" record of past relationships, which is widely visible to "le tout Paris." Minnelli's direction reveals her knowledge in the poignant outburst once Tonton confesses that he loves the young girl. Her intensity here, that of the angry child within the maturing young woman, conveys her feelings not only about his love, which would ignore her distaste for a courtesan's life but also about how badly she would be wounded if he were to leave her. Here the film is once again faithful to the novel.

Gigi's conflicted passion—she both loves Gaston and hates him for wanting to seal her fate as a courtesan—which leads to her accepting his offer to be his mistress, is an instance of the movie's questioning of how to cope with and confront troubling phenomena. In this psychoanalytic reading of repressed incestual/incestuous desire, such scenes alternate with those celebrating womanizing and prohibited passion and have the viewer reflect on problems that endure today.

Minnelli's editing of the musical part enables the viewer/listener to enjoy popular tunes and to ponder the characters' emotions, sensations, and thinking at critical times in the film. As indicated above, the addition of the roué Honoré, especially his dangerous, charming renditions of "Thank Heaven for Little Girls" both at the beginning and end of the film seems to enclose, indeed enshrine and glorify, the patriarchal exploitation of females of all ages as sexual objects: womanizing is more than ok.

Minnelli's portrayal of Lachaille Sr., however, further testifies to the film's nuances, which engage the viewer in reflection on the exploiter's degree of awareness and contrition in that he seems to regret, at least years later, his treatment of Alvarez. This ambiguity in Honoré invites the viewer's comparison with Gaston since it appears in his earlier conversation with his nephew whose first offer Gigi initially rejects. Honoré describes having "the door slammed" when he left Mamita for others. Later in the film, he displays a preference for her over a younger woman when he forgoes the latter, joins Mamita at the table in Trouville, and with great affection re-engages with her in the beautiful "I Remember it Well."

Minnelli creates complexity in the film's maternal images with three women: Aunt Alicia, Andrée (Gigi's biological mother, a minor performer in the Opéra comique), and especially Grandmother Alvarez. The latter's nickname, Mamita, highlights the Spanish identity she cultivates but especially the motherly role she plays as the principal caregiver. She enforces, for example, tough-love rules dictating her granddaughter's behavior, for instance, that she visits Aunt Alicia every Tuesday and wears her Sunday coat.

While highlighting Mamita's role, Minnelli appears to simplify the role of Colette's Andrée, Gigi's biological mother, reducing her to comic relief. An abject figure in the novel with important ramifications for its messages, as discussed in Chapter 3 in connection with Kristeva's theory of abjection, she does not appear at all in the movie. The listener hears her only as a voice whose singing seems to annoy, leading Alvarez to shut it out by closing the door.

Susan Smith recognizes a subtle effect of this part of the soundtrack.[3] Beyond the comedy, there is another level of meaning in the singing, enriching the overall messages of the film, especially on the exploitation of women. In the context of the courtesan milieu forcing many women to sell their bodies to create a satisfying life, if only financially, Andrée has chosen to pursue the music she loves rather than marry a wealthy man for whom she did not care. Smith hears pleasure in Andrée's voice as she practices, showing the possibility of other options for women without financial resources—the subject underlying Gigi's and Gaston's dilemma dealing with mistress versus marital status and the implicit incest taboo. In other words, women in the courtesan milieu, like Andrée, can find other ways to make a living, though it is difficult.

While this element of the film's soundtrack seems minor and unrelated in an explicit way to the topic of incest, Smith's insights into it reveal a depth of meaning in the movie that Minnelli creates inadvertently. Having alluded only to the comic effect of Andrée's offstage singing and to the fact that reducing her role serves to underline the grandmother's role as Gigi's caregiver, he appears unaware of the subtle manner in which the film suggests other options for intelligent women in the demi-monde. Smith's analysis notices how the singer's voice conveys love for her music and a sense of commitment to values different from those of the patriarchal courtesan world. The examination of Andrée's significant role aptly includes reference to Gigi's own comment in response to her grandmother's critique of her mother's choices, "She seems happy," in both film and novel. This is further evidence of the young girl's intelligent observations throughout, especially her resistance to the demi-monde lifestyle.

Kristeva's theories on motherhood illuminate Gigi's positive responses both to her biological mother's choice of work over marriage and to her actual caregiver, her grandmother. The young girl's behavior in successfully pursuing her desire for Gaston shows, in Kristevan terms, that she has found a way to reconnect with the mother, understood as the necessary step in developing the ability to live viscerally, in body as well as mind.

Beyond the presence of the maternal in Andrée's singing, a significant example of the musical elements of the film also has the viewer/listener consider how to cope with and confront an exploitative world: Gaston's song in the concluding scenes, as I will show. The attentive viewer notices that his uncle's congratulating him on buying Gigi as his mistress while also noting that her youth ensures a longer time for pleasure, prompts the nephew to reflect and/or contributes to his ongoing reflection. He decides to take her back to her home. Like Andrée's singing, his, in the scene which follows, reveals an attitude different from that of the patriarchal demi-monde encouraging the exploitation of young girls like Gigi. His point of view is at odds with "Thank Heaven for Little Girls," potentially pedophiliac and definitely incestual in the movie's context.

Faithful to Colette's novel in this, Minnelli creates a complicated young gigolo who is bored and melancholy in the demi-monde, but not so in the boring and nondescript apartment that is the primary setting for the film. Thus, the director faithfully adapts the original narrative, highlighting Gaston's love for Gigi, Alvarez, and their home, including chamomile tea and cassoulet. These are unusual, low-key pleasures for such a Casanova in both versions. He comes to realize during and via his song that he should not continue to contribute to her grooming to become his mistress. Instead, he will pursue a way to offer her the possibility of being more of his equal, that is, a socially respected form of adulthood as his wife, despite the ambiguity created by the hovering of the incest taboo.

One of the best examples of Minnelli's use of music to slow down the plot and encourage the viewer's reflection on the couple's dilemma is in fact Gaston's final song as he contemplates his choices. The scene is striking in its setting of the city of light after sunset with the handsome lover in his top hat, as discussed more in detail in the following text .

While it does not call attention to the positive ethics embodied in Gaston's concluding number with its moving, lyrical qualities, the earlier setting in Maxim's also slows down the narrative and engages thinking via freeze-frames. They serve as contrast to the lover's break with his former values and make more prominent the gossip and potentially destructive aspects of "le tout Paris" as the wealthy clients discuss the latest ephemeral romances.

The movie's principal setting, Gigi's modest apartment, contributes to the compelling them of resistance to that exploitative demi-monde. Its walls are the red-color fitting for a growing passion bent on mutual respect despite the history of unequal power relations of child and parent, that is, incestual love, as well as the threat of biological incest. The viewer often sees the young girl at home in the setting that dominates the film holding her cat as they give or receive comfort from each other. This emphasizes affection and mirrors Colette's own love for her feline pets. In fact, Minnelli makes literal use of the looking glass in such scenes as we see Gigi peering at her image as she ponders her identities. Such details in the form of the film fine-tune its ambivalent messages, which include incestual/incestuous passion, on the one hand, and marriage/domesticity on the other. Like Colette, Minnelli's vision is not primarily cynical and pessimistic, especially in conveying the couple's growing, maturing feelings for each other.

Movie critics like those writing on the novel misread Minnelli's mixed messages about womanizing, love, marriage, and the implicit prohibition that is the topic of this book. While Kristeva's theories indirectly illuminate my reading of the film, her comments on it are minimal. Most important among them are her observations that (1) Minnelli's style, like Colette's, is allusive and quick-paced (2) that Leslie Caron's Gigi, while both elegant and mischievous, fails to convey the subtleties of the novel's heroine and (3) that the movie tends to portray the perceived frivolousness of French culture in its transformation of music hall entertainment into an authentic American musical film comedy in which humor overshadows Colette's delicate ellipsis.[4] Kristeva recognizes the strength of its style but, like other commentators, misreads the movie in her remarks on Caron's Gigi and its supposed portrayal of French lack of seriousness.

Smith is an exception as explained above but like most others, she too does not consider the significant implications of the incest taboo. Stephen Harvey labels Minnelli's work "devious" and "unsavory" because of the disguise of the theme of grooming for a life of prostitution in an appearance of childlike innocence and eventual marriage. Yet, he notes the directorial genius, the contradictions in his films, their substance, melancholy, and unexpected depth of feeling and observation.[5] Like many viewers, he has difficulty interpreting the ambiguities of Minnelli's movies, including *Gigi's*. The ambiguous nuances and development in the lovers' characters harbor unconscious drives—in other words, incestuous/incestual desires.

Others also recognize the movie's strengths without noticing such repressed longings. Raymond Bellour, for example, emphasizes the subtle links among the film's complicated images.[6] These create a coherent focus on the theme of "little girls" and constitute in his mind "classic film," though his reliance on Christian Metz's terminology is jargonistic. Bellour's breakdown of the plot, music, setting, and so on, does, however, provide useful material for an analysis of the movie.

Albert Johnson is among the best who take the film seriously and recognize Minnelli's ability to reveal his characters' complex psychology, though he too ignores the impact of the incest taboo. He writes:

> Minnelli's use of the lyric hero in *Gigi* is brilliantly achieved, making Gaston more important than anyone else in the film. Gaston's long soliloquy and melodic utterances of the title song, excellent in conception and mood, are followed, later in the film, by a reprise of the number in purely photographic and musical terms. The orchestrations and camera elaborate Gaston's top-hatted silhouette against the nighttime streets and fountains of Paris as he roams, disconsolately silent, stunned by first love. It is a musical number unlike anything else ever seen upon the screen, an Impressionist mood-piece haunted by the sketches of Lautrec.[7]

Here, Johnson insightfully emphasizes the strength of Minnelli's direction, the cinematography, and the shift in foregrounding Gaston. In doing so, the critic helps to raise vital questions about both the film's faithfulness to the spirit of Colette's novel and her much-disputed feminism.

The examination of Colette's virile identifications sheds light on the movie's emphasis on Gaston's role as well as on Kristeva's theories. In the analysis in the newly translated essay, "Neither Depression nor Perversion: Colette in Bloom," which I include in this volume, she examines the ways in which the novelist not only provides the perspectives of both child and parent but also how identification with Chéri indirectly surfaces in the eponymous novel and especially in *The End of Chéri*. She writes:

> Beyond avenging a cheating husband, Colette's pen also takes aim at the young man morbidly attached to a false mother, a man thrown outside time and consequently destined to die. But *La Fin de Chéri*, this novel so intent on getting even, is not so much concerned with the real figure of the incestuous son. At this time, her relationship with Bertrand is over and Maurice Goudeket has already entered the writer's life. In fact, considering her many affirmations of a virile identification, one can see a masculine version of Colette in the character Chéri. The narrator projects herself onto Léa and also onto Fred through her relation to the former. This complementary movement, which she outlines in exploring the perverse connection, has her confront in another way her phallic aspirations and their inevitable failure.
>
> Yes, she will be the man who fully satisfies her mother [...][8]

While this passage discusses neither *Gigi* nor Minnelli's adaptation, it recognizes that one identifies with both females and males, which is not surprising, particularly in the case of a bisexual author. Kristeva's analysis of how Colette projects herself onto Chéri, as well as onto Léa enables an interpretation of Minnelli's adaptation, which earlier critics have not considered. Namely, the attentive spectator will understand the fact that the director recognizes an example of Colette's virile identification in his choosing the male character, Gaston, not the female, to reveal the value of heterosexual marriage in what may be the strongest scene in the film.

Emanuel Levy's review notices important visual elements in the movie, including this remarkable scene, which serve to highlight its implicit theme of incest though he does not mention this directly.[9] He insightfully states: "In Minnelli's Paris, statues of mythological rape loom over Gigi as she ponders the Parisians' sex drive, and the Beaux Arts fixtures of the Pont Alexander are presented when Gaston expresses his feelings over the new Gigi." Both the statues depicting sexual aggression and the bridge cherubs are related to the prohibited passion at the center of the film as well as the questions it poses on the treatment of women and children.

Without raising the topic of incest, Dan Seeger points out an example demonstrating the movie's apparent celebration of the exploitation of young females: "Gaston's typically cavalier way with women has led one of his discarded conquests to attempt suicide, a development that is greeted with beaming pride by Honoré, who raises a champagne glass and enthuses, 'May this be the first of many! ' "[10]

His analysis of Honoré's proud behavior calls attention to the ironies of viewing attempted suicide as proof of Gaston's skill as Casanova, the death of a human being in the Parisian demi-monde. One also notices the irony in Honoré's name. This critic's analysis is right on the mark as are Elizabeth Ladenson's observations of such behavior in Lachaille Sr. Her article, "Colette aux Etats-Unis," ostensibly on Minnelli's distortions, in fact, serves to highlight the musical's rendering of the hint of incest hovering in the wings, in this and other ways remaining faithful to the spirit of the novel it adapts to the screen, as I am demonstrating.[11] I include a lengthy discussion of her article here, despite its many inaccurate observations, because they enable consideration of several significant elements of the movie's form and content, including reviews related to the topic of prohibited desire.

Ladenson notes, for instance, that Minnelli's adaptation makes a meaningful change in adding scenes absent in the novel between Gigi's accepting Gaston's offer to be his mistress and his offer of marriage. This critic sees these episodes lengthening the time taken to reach his decision as a distortion in their focus on the young girl's surprising behavior as well as on the male characters. She concludes that they take the attention away from Gigi herself as resisting courtesan life and betray the spirit of Colette's text and her feminism.

On looking at this change more closely, one finds that this is not a distortion of the novel but rather that the film like the book on which it is based incorporates the novelist's values to the extent that Minnelli has Gaston both fall in love for the first time and in a manner that enables him to see the folly of his earlier ways. In other words, he understands that she is much more than courtesan material. It is not, however, that Minnelli betrays the values underlying the novel nor does he portray Gigi in a negative manner because of her decision—as Ladenson would have us believe—given that the young woman convincingly does this out of love for him. Minnelli's film, in lengthening the time between Gigi's accepting the role of mistress and Gaston's marriage offer, emphasizes the moving love between the two. Slowing the plot down in this way makes the characters' changing feelings more credible in the movie: Gigi comes to believe that she would be more unhappy without Gaston than with him, as she states, and Gaston will realize that Gigi should not be reduced to the status of courtesan.

Other of Ladenson's observations have merit but do not recognize the degree and significance of Gaston's boredom and his insights into and love for the "real" Gigi, a beautiful young girl who is an autonomous and intelligent human being. These components in him help recreate the spirit of Colette's novel and illustrate the complexity of her version of feminism. That is to say, while she normally focuses on the psychology of women, she also examines that of men including their non-sexist values and behavior. Thus, she is not tied to an identity politics that restricts feminism to one gender. In this novel, for example, Colette has Gaston see that he should marry Gigi. In other words, the novelist creates complex male characters with significant non-sexist values, including not only Gaston but also Chéri in the eponymous novel, as well as the father in *La Maison de Claudine*. The novelist does not, however, develop Lachaille as does Minnelli in a way that slows down the chronology of events leading to the offer of marriage. In fact, in the novel, he proposes right after her acceptance of the status of mistress, as Ladenson points out, though her judgment that the change in sequence is a distortion is not valid in my reading of the film.

Her sense that the United States created a mythological France of erotic traffic in very young girls is interesting and worth examining in an effort to understand better this culture. In other words, she suggests that the mythological France has incestual if not incestuous desire at its center, in the sense in which I am using the term. This may be true considering French culture's fixation on the gamine and the child in the country's cultural production.[12] I will return below to the subject of the relations between the two countries in the history of ideas, especially in the way in which Colette's thinking shapes this film as well as in Kristeva's take on her virile identifications.

Ladenson's revelation of Lerner's and Minnelli's comments on the source they followed in turning Lachaille Sr. into Gaston's uncle and expanding his role uncovers elements important for a better understanding of both the novel and its adaptation. As the critic states, while the direction, as well as the screenplay, and lyrics, hide the way in which they copy elements of the plot from Jacqueline Audry's French adaptation of *Gigi* in 1949, they also raise important questions for a comparison of the American musical and Colette's novel.

For example, Minnelli notes both Colette's minimal treatment of Lachaille Sr. in her narrative and Audry's expansion of his part in her French adaptation. From my point of view, in context, the very brief mention of the father in the novel is part of the unconscious subtext in which the incest taboo raises its ugly head if only for seconds. In other words, Colette's inclusion is significant *because* it is minimal—the brevity of it signals its unconscious nature, that is, something one must repress, at least in part.

Ladenson's mention of Minnelli's adding Lachaille Sr. to the last scene at Maxim's supports my argument in that it highlights the father's emphasis on Gigi's youth. She is appealing because still a girl available for future sexual pleasure as Honoré implies in his comments to Gaston.

"Colette aux Etats-Unis" is also critical of mainstream US culture, seeing it as not capable of reading Colette properly and therefore distorting her thoughts in Minnelli's adaptation. Ladenson is reductive here. I include her remarks, however, because her unfounded criticisms serve to raise questions about opposing perspectives, enabling a fuller understanding of the film and novel. Ladenson is unaware of the excellent analyses of Colette by critics from the United States. These include Tama L. Engelking, discussed in Chapter 3,[13] as well as the film critic and director Albert Johnson quoted above. Both offer compelling analyses of the film as a powerful adaptation of Colette's writing.

Ladenson reveals the greed in Minnelli's and especially Lerner's work to withdraw Audry's film from circulation in the States. They bought the rights to the film, enabling them to ensure the viability of their own version, though this may not have been necessary given the fact that movies in foreign languages do not normally claim much of the American market.

"Colette aux Etats-Unis" sees Minnelli's film catering to Americans' interest in the geography of Paris but not its history. As Johnson points out, however, among the movie's merits is the visual power of its recreation of the Belle Epoque and its courtesan culture of the time: it recreates "an environment of elegance and imaginary innocence."[14]

Despite Ladenson's comment that Colette writes for the stage and not the screen, her novels are admirably suited to adaptation for both the theatre and the movies to the degree that they focus on ideas and images communicable to a broad audience. In other words, *Gigi* is an example of literature as popular culture understood in the best sense. No less an expert on film than Max Ophuls in fact thinks Colette's novel is a masterpiece and well-suited to adaptation. Alain Ferrari's excellent article, "Mon dernier voyage terrestre: Colette et le cinema" quotes Ophuls's invitation to Colette to have him adapt *Gigi* to the screen. Having collaborated with the novelist on the film *La Divine*, he writes to her, speaking of *Gigi*, "I want to make this film." Ferrari's article also contributes convincing arguments for finding Minnelli's version better than Audry's in adapting the novel to the screen and zeroes in on his direction of Leslie Caron's portrayal of the combination of suffering and astonishment in Gigi as she matures as well as the joy of and love for the young in the movie taken as a whole, problematic though it may be.[15] Finally, Ladenson is wrong about grandmother's and Alicia's belief that marriage is not possible. They do see this choice, at least in the last segments of the film, revealing the two women with their eyes quite aware of the couple's imminent marriage and for this reason contributing to the movie's lively climax.

Thus, Ladenson neither notices many of the nuances of Minnelli's adaptation nor gives serious attention to the incest taboo lurking in both the novel and film. Her critique, however, as I have shown, calls attention to significant elements of both form and content.

As for the question of the adaptation's faithfulness to the spirit of Colette's text overall, the critics' reviews are mixed, with the best analyses responding in the affirmative and confirming my reading. There are differences in both their sense of the nature of the author's strengths apart from the film and their evaluation of the movie as an adaptation. Pierre Schneider, to take one of the best examples of the former, recognizes the animality and verbal artistry in Colette's writing in general (see Chapter 1).[16]

This text of Colette's, however, conveys less intense physical drives than her other writing, for example, *Chéri* and *La Maison de Claudine* discussed in Chapters 1 and 2. One recalls, to take three examples, Chéri's murmur and moan of "an entire tender, animal song" after a second kiss. The recipient of those kisses, Léa, experiences a loss of dignity as a human as she anticipates sex as a dismembered half of an animal cut apart who will then fuse with another as a single, previously severed beast.[17] In *La Maison de Claudine,* the narrator speaks of "that […] most disturbing of instincts"—the apt expression serving as the subtitle of this book in my translation—in connection with her young daughter's anxious question about when it is appropriate for a man to put his arm around a woman.[18]

Both Colette's and Minnelli's *Gigi* use the cat to evoke the connection between the animal and the human, but in a more delicate way than in examples from the earlier novels stressing the force of the physical. As mentioned earlier, the director has Gigi often holding her pet as they comfort each other. The film makes use of the mirror more than once to show Gigi holding the animal and considering her image. She tries to understand her mind as well as to assess her looks as she matures, a behavior typical of a female in love at an early age. Once she decides to become Gaston's mistress and before he offers her marriage, Minnelli photographs her with her cat peering into the mirror as if questioning her identity somewhat like Léa who feared the loss of her sense of self in contemplating her desire and imminent sex with Chéri.[19] Gigi proceeds in this scene to sing, as if to the pet, "Say a prayer for me tonight," mentioning her youth and death ("too young to die") just before she goes out with Gaston for her first night as his mistress. In Minnelli's remarkable adaptation, the cat's image serves to connect the animality of Colette's texts to the film and her biography, given her love for animals, especially the feline, including big cats. Her chapter "Bâ-tou" in *Claudine's House* indicates a preference for them, given their greater honesty compared to humans. I include Sue Super's fine drawing of a lion at the end of my book for this reason.

Beyond her love for animals, the movie insightfully dramatizes vital elements in Colette's life, which help uncover the deep-seated reasons for the hovering of the incest taboo in Minnelli's adaptation and in her novels after 1903, the publication date of her final Claudine narrative. I am referring to the problematic relationship with her first husband, Willy. It is likely that the Claudine novels which he pressured her to write and then published as his own, haunted her in the forties when she wrote the novel. Willy's ghost surfaces clearly in the film's focus on the child Gigi's developing love for the father figure Gaston as well as in the significant portrayal of Andrée's choice of work over marriage discussed above. Minnelli introduces the phantom of this first husband early on in Sem's drawing of Colette, Willy, and the actor, Polaire, another of his love objects, in the opening of the movie as the credits appear.

As an adaptation, the film also affirms the contribution Colette makes to the development of the genre of the novel as a middle-class form. Her influence on Minnelli and his musical film emphasizes the ways in which women have played a critical role in reinventing fiction and its connections to cinema and popular culture as much more than an escape.

Given the director's skill in adapting Colette's focus on the psychology of women and the female love object at an early age to the screen, the film has vital ramifications for feminist studies, and especially psychoanalytic theory in France and the United States In my consideration of the novel as inspiration for Minnelli's movie, French models emerge as an important influence on American thought. This appears to contradict my earlier statement that the film sets in motion a myth about the erotic in France, in other words, the movie has an impact on the culture of France. Influence, however, often flows in both directions as it does here. The author of *Gigi* provides insight into the power of internal, psychological forces in women's development and their impact on social transformation, that is, Gigi's engagement in coping with incestual desire and womanizing including the influence she exerts on Gaston. The emphasis on women's psychology surfaces in Minnelli's adaptation and signals in my reading the way in which mental life takes precedence over the strength of external causes.

One could read the novel's ending in marriage as acceptance of the domesticity required by the culture. In context, however, marriage is a way for Gigi to subvert the courtesan lifestyle that is the norm in the demi-monde in which she lives and to have Gaston in a manner that is not antithetic to her psychology.

In conclusion, Colette's focus on psychology in *Gigi* is part of the dialogue between French and American models. One of my earlier books examines a tendency in the more pragmatic thinking of the United States to focus on external causes, especially the social contract and the marketplace, and to disparage non-cognitive psychology, in the form of the psychoanalytic theory of the French feminists, particularly Kristeva. I refer to the concluding chapter "Europhilia-Europhobia" of her 2002 *Intimate Revolt* and her novel, *The Enchanted Clock* as influential texts in this dialogue.[20] Here, Colette's *Gigi*, the inspiration for Minnelli's adaptation, is an early example of the influence of French models that help to shape feminist thinking in the United States, including that of this director.

Notes

1 *Gigi*, directed by Vincente Minnelli (1958; Burbank, CA: Warner Home Video, 2000), DVD.

2 See my *Language and Politics in Julia Kristeva: Literature, Art, Therapy* (Albany, New York: State University of New York Press, 2006), pp. 6, 65–66, 83–86, 91.

3 See Susan Smith, "Singing Outside the Frame: The Female Voice-off in Gigi (Minnelli, 1958)," *CineAction*, no. 72 (spring 2007): 32+. *Gale Literature Resource Center.* https://archive.org/stream/CineAction.072/CineAction.072_djvu.txt.

4 Julia Kristeva, *Colette*, trans. Jane Marie Todd (New York: Columbia University Press, 2004), p. 355.

5 See Stephen Harvey, "Darkening Beauty: On Some Films of Vincente Minnelli," *MoMA*, vol. 2, no. 2 (Autumn, 1989): 14–16. https://www.jstor.org/stable/4381091.

6 See Raymond Bellour, "To Analyze, to Segment," *Quarterly Review of Film Studies*, vol. 1, no. 3 (August 1976): 331–353.
7 Albert Johnson, "The Films of Vincente Minnelli: Part II," *Film Quarterly*, vol. 12, no. 3 (Spring, 1959): 39.
8 See Kristeva's article, "Neither Depression nor Perversion: Colette in Bloom," (this issue): 93–105.
9 Emanuel Levy, "Gigi (1958): Minnelli Oscar-Winning Musical," *Cinema 24/7* (July 17, 2006). https://emanuellevy.com/review/gigi-1958-4/.
10 See Dan Seeger, "Œuvre: Minnelli: *Gigi*," *SpectrumCulture* (December 12, 2013). https://spectrumculture.com/2013/12/12/oeuvre-minnelli-gigi/.
11 Elizabeth Ladenson, "Colette aux Etats-Unis," *Cahiers Colette*, vol. 19 (1997): 217–228.
12 See, for example, *Girls in French and Francophone Literature and Film*, ed. Daniela Di Cecco (Leiden, The Netherlands: Brill/Rodopi, 2015); and Abby Lockett, 2015, "From Déesse to Idée: The Woman-Child in French New Wave Film," Capstone Research, The University of Texas at Austin.
13 See "Crossing Borders with Colette's *Gigi*," *The French Review*, vol. 93, no. 3 (March 2020): 108.
14 Albert Johnson, "The Films of Vincente Minnelli: Part II," 38.
15 See Alain Ferrari, "Mon dernier voyage terrestre: Colette et le cinéma," in L'Herne: *Colette*, ed. Gérard Bonal & Frédéric Maget (Paris: L'Herne, 2011), p. 165.
16 Pierre Schneider, "Paris: Fresh Look at Colette's Work," *The New York Times* (April 9, 1973). https://archive.nytimes.com/www.nytimes.com/books/99/10/17/specials/colette-fresh.html.
17 Colette, *Chéri and The End of Chéri*, trans. Rachel Careau (New York: W.W. Norton & Co., 2022), pp. 30, 130.
18 Colette, "*My Mother's House*," in *My Mother's House and Sido*, trans. Una Vincenzo Troubridge & Enid McLeod (New York: Farrar, Straus & Giroud, 2002), p. 138.
19 Colette, *Chéri and The End of Chéri*, p. 29.
20 *Kristeva in America: Re-imagining the Exceptional* (London and New York: Palgrave, 2020), pp. 43–77. https://doi.org/10.1007/978-3-030-39912-6.

Chapter 5

FAR FROM THE FATHER OF PERSONAL PRE-HISTORY: WESTMORELAND'S *COLETTE*

Colette's relationship to the first husband prominent in her life and writing, the infamous Willy, Henry Gauthiers-Villars, dominates in Wes Westmoreland's eponymous biographical period film of 2018.[1] The movie garnered many nominations and kudos for its direction, Dominic West's, Keira Knightley's, and Denise Gough's performances, the costumes, and its contributions to LGBTQ cinema. It also won an international award for Thomas Adès's music. Yet critics, especially scholarly readers, have overlooked or given only a superficial reading of the film.

The cursory reviews tend to focus on the dominant presence of Willy as well as the identity politics of 2018, without agreeing on whether these elements are strengths or weaknesses. The reviews, however, implicitly bring to light the principal questions Westmoreland raises, as I will show.

Colette limits itself primarily to her early years, especially to the ramifications of her marriage to Willy. Not a weakness of the film, this limitation selects the events that unlock a better understanding of her autofiction and the incestual desire driving it. In my psychoanalytic reading, Westmoreland poses vital questions on the sources of her writing and life, namely the parent–child relationship, its sexual aspects, and its implications for complex identity politics.

Julia Kristeva's theories on the importance of both the father of personal or individual pre-history and masculine identifications in Colette's life and work contribute to my approach to the movie. While she does not mention it, those who do analyze the film often speak of Dominic West's apparent overshadowing of Keira Knightley's portrayal of the author, as in the case of Louis Jourdan's performance seeming to outshine that of Leslie Caron discussed in my preceding chapter on Vincente Minnelli's adaptation. In both cases, these critics speak of the dominance of the male figures as if they distort the thought and life of Colette, and thus minimize the female agency she promoted.[2]

Unlike the father of psychoanalysis, Sigmund Freud, Kristeva focuses on female psychology in her theories on the child's early encounters with a male parent who is androgynous, particularly in his behavior. According to her, the father figure plays a vital role in a young girl's development in the sense that if his authority includes the nurturing love that is more often associated with the mother, the child will be better able to function as a speaking subject in her own right. Thus, it is important that such a complex figure, called the father of personal pre-history in Freud, make his presence felt as the girl acquires a knowledge of language.[3] In my reading of her biography and the novels drawing on it, Colette's biological father arguably functions in this way in his foundational relationship with his daughter. Her attachment to Willy as a father figure appears out of this earlier affection.

Colette portrays Jules-Joseph, the former Zouave soldier who lost his leg during a military campaign in Italy, as both an authority figure and a nurturing presence in *La Maison de Claudine*, examined in Chapter 2. With weaknesses and serving as a foil to the more prominent Sido, her mother, in that volume, he nevertheless plays a positive role as an adoring and adored father and husband. A good example appears in the affectionate description of the sound of his crutch, which accompanied her childhood and youth, "rocking" (my translation) and soothing the young Colette as might a mother.[4] Another instance appears in the same eponymous chapter, where he displays his love in unwarranted "jealousy" over his wife's encounters with local shopkeepers as she does her shopping for the evening's dinner. The narrator makes clear that she feels great affection for her father and his devotion to her mother despite Colette's critique of male/female relations in her writing elsewhere.

Later, in *Sido*, in terms that are moving for both her and the reader, the narrator reveals her discovery that Jules-Joseph was a failed writer. The pages of the book he intended to write include only the words dedicating it to his wife.[5]

John Anderson's review of the film suggests that the two men are not only both failed writers but also static personalities. Without mentioning Jules-Joseph who is also resistant to change, the critic's observation that Willy is unable to develop as he engages with his dynamic wife signals the likelihood that the marriage can never succeed. While the emphasis on the way one may choose a love object who replays the original one is a well-known cliché of Freudian theory, the similarities between biological father and first husband are relevant for an understanding of the specifics of Colette's struggle for autonomy as I will explain.[6]

In the article included in this volume, "Neither Depression nor Perversion: Colette in Bloom," Kristeva analyzes not only Colette's biological father's endearing qualities but also her masculine identifications with him and in the characters she creates. In *Chéri*, as Chapter 1 explains based on the French Bulgarian's analysis, the author projects herself onto the father to achieve union with the mother.[7]

A fuller analysis of characteristics linking the biological father and Willy, including the description "the incestuous harmonics with the father accumulate" appears in the volume *Colette* in Kristeva's trilogy *Female Genius*.[8] In the in-depth approach for which she is famous, she emphasizes the increasing recognition of the affection the author felt for Jules-Joseph and the ways in which his failed attempt at writing shaped her own relationship to composition. In this context, Willy's dominant presence in Westmoreland's film appropriately emphasizes the function of a sexualized paternal source at the center of the psychic formations underlying Colette's writing.

Judith Thurman's fine biography also recognizes the ways in which Willy is a father figure who resembles Jules-Joseph, especially his failure as a writer.[9] She includes examples documenting both the strong love between parent and child and more negative characteristics of their relationship, at least two of which connote exploitation and incest: "After the Captain's death, Colette had to recognize, if only dimly, that Willy's obsessive philandering and Jules Colette's single-minded fidelity were two sides of the same coin, which left her, in both cases, feeling abandoned and desexed." In other words, the two "fathers," in Thurman's reading, loved and abused her in a way that had consequences for her sexuality: the husband's womanizing and the father's exclusive passion for his wife, which often made him indifferent to his daughter.

Thus, the male protagonists' performances are not weaknesses in either Westmoreland's or Minnelli's film. Here, the strength of West's acting in the context of both the movie and Colette's biography aptly conveys the vital, problematic function of the father or parental figure and prohibited desire, which shapes much of the author's fiction. It does so without overshadowing Knightley's remarkable performance.

The movie's plot presents Colette's early infatuation with the older man straightforwardly and without introducing the problem of incest. The dialogue and cinematography, however, soon reveal how the difficulties that develop in her attempts to free herself from him go beyond a period film's depiction of a stereotypical romance at the turn of the twentieth century and conceal incestual desire. This is particularly the case once Willy exploits her in plagiarizing the Claudine novels. *Colette* explores a parent–child relationship buried in the love story of the sophisticated womanizer from Paris who seduces a beautiful young girl from the French countryside. Furthermore, such a rapport, a vital subtext, illuminates Colette's writing, particularly in the three novels examined in this book, as well as shedding light on the enduring problem of infantilization and abuse in power relations in couples today.

Beyond her literary criticism and theory, Kristeva as a practicing psychoanalyst recognizes the presence of the harmful effects of treating a love object as a child. In the following quotation from her book on the novelist, she begins by making clear that she is not speaking of incest per se but rather of the ramifications resulting from treating a partner as if she or he were a child—I add, as Westmoreland depicts Willy's treatment of Colette in the film. She writes:

> Not to be confused with the *reality* of incest and the psychic wounds it inflicts on the children who are its victims, the *unconscious incestuous fantasy* participates in our essentially perverse sexuality, which can even determine the choice of partners and fix them in archaic relationships of the parent-child type (*incestual*, in other words), which exert an influence over the couple that is as jubilant as it is risky and inexorable.[10]

Her comment acknowledges the complexity of such relationships, suggesting the joy but more so the increasing danger and difficulty Colette encounters in her engagement with Willy and in the attempts to extricate herself from him. Other research in psychology, cognitive behavioral, more common in the United States than psychoanalysis, also recognizes the widespread, enduring problem of such incestual relations. Robert Epstein, for example, examines this issue in a recent broad study of the harmful effects of treating a love object as a child.[11]

Throughout his film, Westmoreland subtly depicts Colette as someone who is not yet an adult in her relationship with the much older man, alluding to the incestual desire driving her psyche and writing and thus to the problem named by both Kristeva and Epstein. An early scene at the Parisian salon where Willy introduces his new wife, for instance, has a guest inquire if the young girl is his love child.

As in Minnelli's film discussed in Chapter 4, spanking also links the beloved woman to a child. About to lock her up to continue writing after the success of *Claudine à l'école* in the new country house he has bought for her, Willy introduces the image of the teacher threatening to punish his young student if she does not obey. When he asks her what her teacher would do in such a situation, she responds that he would "put her over his knee and tan her hide."[12]

In the context of *Claudine à l'école*, the first in the Claudine series and focused on her schoolgirl experiences, the references to the father figure as schoolmaster resonate in a movie depicting the difficulties of the author to acquire agency over her life and become the woman Colette rather than to remain Willy's child and student. Furthermore, her husband has the author dress as Claudine to enable him to perform sexually as he had with another object of his desire, Meg. In the end, he admits to being impotent despite these attempts at infantilizing his lovers in seeking arousal.

Colette's future lover, the Russian aristocrat Missy, advises later in the film that she needs to go beyond her identity as "Claudine." I return to this partner's complex role, including more direct links to incestual desire below.

The context stressing the image of a schoolgirl also suggests how the frequent use of animals in the film's images and dialogue serves to reveal the author's lack of autonomy one expects in an adult. When left alone for a time at the first salon experience in Paris, a turtle adorning the drawing room draws her attention. Here, the film appropriately connects the budding author's love for animals as she expresses pity for their plight and imagines their desire for grass. On the carriage ride home, she will identify with the turtle, declaring to Willy that it was as bored as she was. Not an isolated case, Westmoreland had introduced the movie with the chirping of birds and a young Colette in the first scene in bed in her Saint-Sauveur-en-Puisaye, Burgundy home along with a pet cat, also used effectively in Minnelli's film. Later scenes continue to allude to the author's lifelong love for animals, for example, showing affection and care for the French bulldog Willy has bought for her.

A final example, most significant in that Missy helps her lover break free of the exploitative "father," appears late in the movie. The aristocratic Russian woman, with whom Colette begins an enduring relationship, points out that Willy may allow her one that is long but keeps her on a leash nonetheless.

The theme of the family appears often in the depiction of the author as a "child" in her struggles to live with the increasingly exploitative "father." Each member of the incestual couple names her as a parent, but irony makes it clear that she is not. For instance, in one of a number of scenes functioning in that way, Willy describes a nuclear family once they enlist the Algerian actor, Polaire, to perform the role of Claudine in the adaptation of *Claudine à l'école* for the stage: "Father, mother, and daughter." Colette cannot play the part of a parent if her husband pulls the strings: he continues to refuse to recognize her as the author of the book. Westmoreland's camera focuses on the image of an ironic family portrait, with Willy referring to "the Claudine trinity" and signaling to Colette that she should sit on his other knee while Polaire sits on his lap. The film introduces this portrait with the author watching her husband's preposterous staging of the Algerian actor's entry into the restaurant on a litter carried in by sparsely and exotically dressed muscular guards. Still playing and half-pretending to be the submissive child/wife who allows herself only this gentle ironic critique to Schwob, the sympathetic friend who works for her husband, she says that Willy is "subtle as ever." She then obeys the signal and joins Polaire on his lap.

This scene exposes the problem that Westmoreland sets in his portrayal of a dominant Willy. Is he a thorn in the flesh who hampers her development for so long and exploits her talent for his own success? Or is he the charismatic entrepreneur whom Colette loves, who is instrumental in her becoming a writer and the collaborator, as he claims, in the Claudine novels? Westmoreland's strength lies in the fact that he engages the spectator in considering both elements in Willy as an authoritarian patriarch *and* individual father of pre-history in the film and Colette's life and writing. The director is faithful to the spirit of her writing in this respect and throughout the movie, as I am arguing.

In another example of the nuanced depiction of infantilization, Colette explodes with anger, shouting that the books were their baby and that he has killed the child, once she learns that Willy has sold the rights to the Claudine series. In other words, she is not able to be an adult mother protecting her offspring. This scene in fact marks the beginning of the complicated process of growing into adulthood, as she asserts herself and finally confronts the exploitative husband and editor.

The performance by the cantomime (the mime George Wague accompanied by song) is the most powerful scene earlier in the film, and in the movie as a whole, with implications for the parent–child relationship as well as for Westmoreland's and Colette's identity politics. Attending the salon event, Colette responds positively, overwhelmed by the male performer's mouthing of "Down by the Salley Gardens," a song written by William Butler Yeats and Herbert Hughes. She says, somewhat inarticulately, "He's mesmerizing." The performer expresses regret over being too young and naïve to engage in the romantic overtures offered, " 'a secret love' to which I would not agree." The mime is androgynous and the position of hands on the back portrays a couple embracing. The camera then reveals the woman off to the side who is singing. Adès's soundtrack powerfully conveys the intensity of the scene and its effect on the spectators, especially Colette, in whom it has clearly struck a nerve.

As in the case of Gigi in Minnelli's film, Westmoreland uses cinematography to highlight an element of abjection in his protagonist, which the author herself conveys more implicitly in the novel. There are moments in the movie when we see Colette grappling with her thoughts and feelings and coping with her incestual relationship with Willy, as in the cantomime scene. Like her novels themselves, the movie conveys degrees of masochism, guilt, fear, and confusion in the protagonist. It is difficult for her to understand let alone act with assurance and take leave of the exploitative "father."

I have discussed the similarities between Kristeva's and Colette's sense of the abject, on the one hand, and Heidegger's idea of dread, on the other, in my Introduction. William V. Spanos's "The Detective and the Boundary: Some Notes on the Postmodern Literary Imagination" draws on Heidegger's elaboration of dread and the uncanny in a way that is parallel to that of Kristeva and Colette in their exploration of abjection.[13] The article's discussion is applicable to Colette's fiction and the protagonist's psychological formation depicted in Westmoreland's film. Spanos shows how the best novels depict the messiness of experience, the anxiety one confronts, and Nature understood as a raw quality in human life resisting efforts to domesticate it. I return to this similarity in Kristeva's, Colette's, and Heidegger's thinking in my conclusion.

In context, the cantomime scene mirrors Colette's "too young and naïve" position vis-à-vis Willy's forceful, paternal character. The voice, mouthed by the mimic, conveys the ambiguities in the author's own, given her bisexuality, and that it is Willy who will claim ownership in publishing the Claudine novels under his name only.

Also ambiguous is the complex identity politics that the performance implies: the androgynous mimic appears to be both male and female physically, the lyrics name a male "child," while the singer is a woman. The remarkable scene thus has implications for the film's contributions to LBGT cinema. Colette's response reveals that the event has struck a nerve in her, implying an intensification in her quest for identity and agency, in other words, a search that is political to the degree that she looks to exercise power as a bisexual adult writer and wife. As Peter Keough puts it, the subtlety of the scene's cinematography including its use of soundtrack conveys "in less than a minute [...] the fluidity of gender roles in the Belle Epoque."[14]

The movie later dramatizes Colette's struggles with sexual orientation in some detail in her attraction to women, for example, in her encounter with the married woman in the first salon scene; in her relationship, including sex, with Georgie, the wealthy American woman; and especially in her serious relationship with Missy. Beyond that of the degree of openness to bisexuality, Westmoreland raises the question of his subject's sexual orientation discussed throughout this book. He indirectly conveys the incestual element and the ways in which the love object, in this case, the Russian aristocrat, constitutes a parent in her behavior.

In its allusions to that prohibited desire, the film focuses on Willy, the person who is the primary relationship in Colette's life and writing, beyond her biological parents. Missy is the other principal instance to the extent that her behavior replays the author's incestual rapport with Sido, on whom I focused in Chapter 2. One of the most compelling scenes depicting such conduct in the film also has the photography highlight the French countryside significant in Colette's biography and fiction. The Russian aristocrat plays the role of a wise mother identified with that landscape, reprising that of the author's biological mother, and clear in this narrative. Missy's crucial, influential advice helps the author to understand that her husband is restraining her "on a leash." Missy also influences Colette's growth into a mature woman by pointing out that she has become stuck in a child's identity as "Claudine," unable to become "Colette." Relevant to this subject, Kristeva cites Colette's depiction of Missy as a maternal figure in her letters and novel, *The Tendrils of the Vine*, including its dedications.[15] Peter Bowen includes a brief mention of the Russian aristocrat's increasingly maternal role in the author's life in his "Who's Who in *Colette*."[16]

Beyond the portrayal of her relations with Missy, further explorations of the author's sexuality vis-à-vis parental figures appear in scenes in the bedroom with Willy and depict the difficulties faced by a woman trying to start intercourse. Such scenes imply that complex double standards restrict women's sexuality in more ways than one. Other examples appear in both early and later discussions between husband and wife about responding to a woman's infidelity in sleeping with someone of the same sex rather than with a man, for instance, in connection with Colette's fictional character Renaud in the Claudine novels.

In this context, the mime scene, a microcosm of the movie, incorporates identity politics not in a way that focuses on teaching a lesson on inclusion but rather that portrays bisexuality and incestual desire. Colette's description of this complex, vital part of being human is "that […] most majestic and disturbing of drives" (my translation), one that requires the careful examination implicit in her novels and Westmoreland's film.[17]

Another captivating mime scene depicting the progress in her struggles with sexual orientation and autonomy as a woman and writer has implications for both versions of the double standard discussed above: initiating sex and infidelity. In this instance, Colette has matured into the adult woman who has started not only a sexual relationship with Georgie but also Missy's engagement in theatre, namely, to perform with her in vaudeville in the Egyptian Dream episode, famous in the author's biography. Replete with orientalism, the performance includes the Russian aristocrat's role as Anubis, the god of funeral rites. The latter resurrects the beautiful Colette as a version of Salome, with a kiss that brings the Moulin Rouge house down in violent protest over sex between two women. Herod's daughter is especially proper in the film given her relevance to the buried incest theme: Salome dances to please her father.

Critics raise the question of the film's identity politics but do not agree on whether it is a strength or a weakness. For some, Westmoreland excels in mobilizing the political climate of 2018 in a movie set more than a century earlier. For others, he distorts the culture of the period portrayed, catering to his audience's taste.[18] In the close reading of the film's subtext attempted here, it is Colette herself who enables Westmoreland to depict a complex identity politics relevant to both the Belle Epoque and 2018. He focuses on a subject whose thinking is ahead of her time.

Westmoreland takes care to include the specifics from her biography, which backs up this judgment. Colette uses masculine pronouns and nicknames documented in her letters to her lover, Missy, an early example of a transgender man. Lewis Corner in his interview with the director, Clémance Michallon, along with Sandra Song in her conversation with Denise Gough, who played the role of Colette's Russian partner, discuss this prescient behavior, including, for example, the use of "Uncle Max" to refer to him. Thus, the film has the spectator consider to what extent its identity politics is faithful to that of the twenty-first century as well as to that of the turn of the twentieth century when the term "transgender" did not exist.[19]

As the film critic Lisa Schwartzbaum explains in her article on Steven Spielberg's *Munich* (2005), "historically based movies are never only about the period in which the story is set or even when the work was made. Movies morph and shift constantly, offering new insights and solaces in relation to the time in which we watch them."[20] The observation is relevant to such movies at their best and to the identity politics of Westmoreland's *Colette* in my reading. As Alex Leininger succinctly explains, "*Colette* looks forward while at the same time looking back."[21]

Near the end of the film, Westmoreland's superb direction of cinematography has the charismatic precursor contemplating her image in a mirror. She speaks of her sense of self as both unchanging ("I am the same") and in flux ("I […] expect […] some commonplace little miracle […] will mend again the necklace of my days") as she reflects on her "deep-set eyes" and the "painted mentor" she observes. Here, the viewer understands that she is reflecting on her troubling struggle for sexual orientation and autonomy as a woman, wife, and writer. The use of mirroring, metaphorical in the earlier cantomime and Moulin Rouge mime episodes, functions here and throughout the film as in Minnelli's *Gigi*. More than the reflecting glass women use to prepare to appear in public, the mirror serves to convey her attempts at self-understanding and interior growth.

Finally, Westmoreland employs Adès's composition for the trumpet, the instrument previously used to signal Willy's character, in the concluding soundtrack. Here, the film ironically calls attention to Colette's achievement in liberating herself, at least in part, from the destructive impact of an incestual relationship.

Ibtisaam has written the best article on *Colette* of which I am aware.[22] In a rare move, this reviewer who was trained as a lawyer and is not a film critic professionally, draws on Kristeva's work as does this book to help understand the author's writing and to evaluate the film. She emphasizes that the author's feminism as portrayed in it is controversial and does not fit into the simplistic identity politics of writers today, as I have been arguing.

Her article, however, has unwarranted criticisms, does not notice many of the film's nuances, and is overly brief, especially on its form, including its cinematography and soundtrack. She nevertheless speaks accurately of both Colette's feminism and her complex relationship with Willy, which is a central element in my thesis on the movie. She writes: "West captivates the audience as a sleazy but witty hustler and the relationship between the two is not a simple foray into the bad, mean husband and his poor suffering wife. In fact, many of the scenes between Willy and Colette display the complexities of a relationship that still contains tenderness despite the continuous betrayals and attempted control."

This relationship helps in making the careful spectator aware of the incest taboo driving the author's behavior and writing in my reading. Without speaking of it directly, Ibtisaam insightfully identifies the "tenderness," "complexities," and "control," which often accompany an incestual rapport, though these alone do not define it. Her article concludes that it is impossible to understand or portray Colette in a movie. While this judgment may be true, it does not sufficiently recognize how helpful Westmoreland is in providing a biographical film that illuminates her novels, particularly *Gigi*'s depiction of a girl's relationship to a much older man and the significance of the author's foundational first marriage.

In the context it provides, the movie along with Kristeva's essay included in this book, makes audible the novelist's voice enabling an understanding of the problematic power dynamics at play in parent–child love relationships then and now. I have shown how Colette understands the incestual/incestuous desire underpinning the couple in complex ways including (1) the older woman and younger man (*Chéri*), (2) the mother and daughter (*La Maison de Claudine*), and (3) the younger woman and the older man (*Gigi*). The psychological formations experienced in childhood and replayed in these compelling narratives have significant consequences for adult lives, particularly for women and their marginalized positions. Colette's writing, "the flesh of the world," in Kristeva's phrase, incorporates existence in words to strengthen women in their struggle for autonomy. Briefly put, as I have shown, her novels do this by creatively juxtaposing multiple perspectives both outside and inside the psyche via her characters and third-person limited narrator. Westmoreland's *Colette* conveys this juxtaposition visually, for example, in the remarkable cantomime scene which portrays a young androgenous person mouthing the voice of another. Here, an attentive viewer will see the young Colette struggling to cope with incestual desire for and resistance to Willy's dominating paternal presence in her life, as discussed above.

Colette's thinking on political issues beyond the couple remains murky and problematic as I read Kristeva's illuminating references to this topic.[23] One remembers the novelist's comment that she knows nothing of those questions and especially her delay in speaking out against the Nazis during World War II until her third husband Maurice Goudeket was in danger of deportation.

Colette's insight into the power dynamics of the couple, however, is clear. My examination of the three novels included in this book, Minnelli's adaptation of *Gigi*, Westmoreland's film focused on her first marriage, and Kristeva's incisive essay included here reveals the novelist's thinking on this topic. In my reading, Kristeva's formulation of the novelist's writing as constituting "existence in the flesh of the world" lies at the heart of the essay and serves to integrate the fiction. The novelist recreates the mind's experience of living viscerally in its environment, a phenomenon originally formulated by Merleau-Ponty, related to Heidegger's "taking-as" and "care," and prominent in the more recent work of Spillers and Judy on literature and the body (see Chapter 1).

Noëlle McAfee writes convincingly on Kristeva's drawing from the German philosopher in her elaboration of the abject as an element in creating a moral vision of difference and respect. "Abject Strangers: Toward an Ethics of Respect" focuses on Heidegger's sense that the anxiety or dread arising from experiences of the uncanny have the potential to develop into Dasein or an authentic creation of self.[24] Kristeva draws on such anxiety in her idea of the abject, emerging out of loss of connection to others and containing within it the capability of birth into a productive subjectivity, which reconnects to others. As her essay included in this volume reveals, Colette's recreation of physical and psychic experience in her writing, grounded in presence, temporal unity, and memory, emerges out of incestuous desires. These longings are perverse in their disturbance of the social contract as well as of proper connections to others. While the novelist does not condone incest, her fiction dramatizes such desires to investigate creativity's relationship or even rootedness in their psychology and affect. In this way, reading Colette changes the way one thinks of incest and its ramifications.

Furthermore, the reference to feminism and its implications for identity politics in the essay is noteworthy in that she and Colette engage in questions of gender and power in ways that are quite different from those we see in the United

States. My reading of the novels as well as of Kristeva's take on them in this book makes clearer that their thinking on this issue is complex and helps to explain the mixed response to the two writers by many multi-culturalists in the United States, indeed, by many Americans in general. Michael Lapointe speculates on the lack of popularity of Colette in the United States—a mixture of positive and negative responses to her writing is more accurate—citing William Gass's view that Americans "though they know a bit about sex [...] prefer not to know about sensuality." Lydia Davis believes it may have to do with Colette's being a woman focusing on love. Lapointe also speaks of her scandalous life including the abusive, incestuous love affair with her stepson, as well as her contradictory stances on both feminism and the Nazi presence in France, all of which may be factors in the mixed response. He includes Edmund White's statement in his blurb on Colette's *Chéri*, that Léa and her young lover "are the most convincing arguments I know of against political correctness in fiction."[25]

My view is that Colette's and Kristeva's thinking on feminism is complex, replete with apparent contradictions, and not a good fit with more pragmatic concerns in the United States, as I have argued in regard to the French Bulgarian in my book, *Kristeva in America*, as well as in my essay on her novel *The Enchanted Clock*.[26] I am using "pragmatic" not in the sense in which philosophy uses the term, for example, in referring to the writing of William James or John Dewey, though there are connections to them. Instead, I use it to refer to a central problem Kristeva raises, the reduction of knowledge to causes outside of the self, divine or moral, and increasingly associated with the marketplace.[27]

In the face of the onslaught of factors outside of the subject, especially economic and consumerist pressures, and the thinking on which they are based, Kristeva and Colette consistently focus on elements within, and the need to understand the psyche more deeply, including the unconscious, incestuous/incestual drives. This examination of Colette's writing including the two films adapting and dealing with her fiction has therefore focused on illuminating the ways her thought contributes to knowledge of the psychology of women in a changing world.

Notes

1 Wash Westmoreland, *Colette* (Los Angeles: Bold Films/Bleeker Street Media, 2018), Amazon Prime Video.

2 See for example Richard Lawson's review in *Vanity Fair* (January 21, 2018). https://www.vanityfair.com/hollywood/2018/01/colette-lizzie-borden-movie-reviews-keira-knightley-chloe-sevigny.

3 See Julia Kristeva, *Tales of Love*, trans. Leon S. Roudiez (New York: Columbia University Press, 1987), pp. 26, 46.

4 Colette, "La Jalousie," in *La Maison de Claudine*, in *Œuvres*, vol. II, ed. Claude Pichois (Paris: Gallimard, 1986).
5 Colette, "*Sido*," in *My Mother's House and Sido*, trans. Una Vicenzo (sic) Troubridge & Enid McLeod (New York: Farrar, Straus & Giroud, 2002), p. 197.
6 See John Anderson, "*Colette*: Literary history with a modern flavor," *The Wall Street Journal* (September 21, 2018): A11. http://pitt.idm.oclc.org/login?url=https://www.proquest.com/newspapers/life-amp-arts-film-review-colette-literary/docview/2109826668/se-2?accountid=14709.
7 See "Neither Depression nor Perversion: Colette in Bloom," (this issue): 93–105.
8 See Julia Kristeva, "*Colette*," in *Female Genius: Life, Madness, Words—Hannah Arendt, Melanie Klein, Colette*, vol. 3, trans. Jane Marie Todd (New York: Columbia University Press, 2004), pp. 184–189.
9 See Judith Thurman, *Secrets of the Flesh* (New York: Alfred A. Knopf, 1999), p. 159.
10 See Julia Kristeva, *Colette*, p. 50.
11 See Robert Epstein, S.D. Bock, M.J. Drew et al, "Infantilization Across the Life Span," *Motivation and Emotion*, vol. 47 (2023): 137–163. https://doi.org/10.1007/s11031-022-09989-4.
12 See p. 53 of the filmscript. https://script-pdf.s3-us-west-2.amazonaws.com/colette-script-pdf.pdf.
13 See William V. Spanos, "The Detective and the Boundary: Some Notes on the Postmodern Literary Imagination Autumn," *Boundary*, vol. 21, no. 1 (Autumn, 1972): 147–168.
14 See Peter Keough's review in *The Boston Globe* (September 26, 2018). https://www.bostonglobe.com/arts/2018/09/26/keira-knightley-takes-writer-pen-colette/1sUkv8wotVjVnWBo9NLqiL/story.html.
15 See Julia Kristeva, *Colette*, pp. 94, 262.
16 See Peter Bowen's "Who's Who in *Colette*" on the Bleeker Street site for the film. https://bleeckerstreetmedia.com/editorial/whos-who-in-colette.
17 Her description "that most [...] disturbing of instincts," which inspired the subtitle of this book, appears in "The Sempstress," *My Mother's House and Sido*, p. 138.
18 See Ibtisaam's "*Colette*: A Film Without Jouissance," in "Medium." https://medium.com/@ibtisaamahmed/colette-a-film-without-jouissance-b7456ad730eb.
19 See Lewis Corner, "*Colette* director Wash Westmoreland on 'the invisible revolution' in his Queer Period Drama," *Gay Times* (December 30, 2018). https://www.gaytimes.co.uk/culture/colette-wash-westmoreland-interview/.
See also Clémance Michallon, "Why *Colette* Will Open the Door to More Queer Period Dramas," *The Independent* (January 12, 2019). https://www.independent.co.uk/arts-entertainment/films/features/colette-keira-knightley-bisexual-dominic-west-movie-queer-period-drama-a8718286.html.
See as well Sandra Song, "Denise Gough Defends her Genderfluid Role as Missy in *Colette*," *Nylon* (September 20, 2018). https://www.nylon.com/articles/denise-gough-colette-interview.
20 See Lisa Schwartzbaum, "The Best Movie About Israel and Gaza Came out 18 Years ago," *The New York Times* (December 24, 2023). https://www.nytimes.com/2023/12/23/opinion/israel-gaza-munich.html.
21 See Alex Leininger, "*Colette* Upends the Biopic's Stodgy Maleness," *PopMatters* (October 17, 2018). http://pitt.idm.oclc.org/login?url=https://www.proquest.com/magazines/colette-upends-biopics-stodgy-maleness/docview/2121182013/se-2.

22 See Ibtisaam, "*Colette*: A Film Without Jouissance," in "Medium." https://medium.com/@ibtisaamahmed/colette-a-film-without-jouissance-b7456ad730eb.

23 See Kristeva, *Colette*, pp. 6, 11, 61–63, 153, 323, 329, 388.

24 Noëlle McKafee, "Abject Strangers: Toward an Ethics of Respect," in *Ethics, Politics, and Difference in Julia Kristeva's Writing*, ed. Kelly Oliver (New York & London: Routledge, 1993), pp. 116–134.

25 See Michael Lapointe's article which cites Gass, Davis, and White, "The Brillance of Colette: A Writer, who Prized the Body Over the Mind," *The New Yorker* (November 15, 2022). https://www.newyorker.com/books/under-review/the-brilliance-of-colette-a-novelist-who-prized-the-body-over-the-mind.

26 See my *Kristeva in America: Re-imagining the Exceptional* (New York: Palgrave, 2021), p. 46 and my "Modernist Trajectories in Time: Kristeva's *The Enchanted Clock*," in *Understanding Modernism: Understanding Kristeva*, ed Maria Margaroni (London: Bloomsbury, 2022). p. 77.

27 See Kristeva's *Intimate Revolt*, trans. Jeanine Herman (New York: Columbia University Press, 2002), p. 262.

NEITHER DEPRESSION NOR PERVERSION: COLETTE IN BLOOM

(Julia Kristeva, trans. Carol Mastrangelo Bové)

Is psychoanalysis too heavy for the alphabet that Colette printed on the very flesh of the world? Is this scholarly terminology too harsh for her "subtle senses," which she transforms into a "word greater than the object"? Maybe this therapy is useless for the craft of her writing. It doesn't claim to "think" but only to follow a "gourmet's quest," given that it's "the everyday fare that sparks her interest."

And what if "monstrous Colette" (Jean Cocteau), her "infernal evil" (Liliane de Pougy), which is said to have "perverted" even "maternal instinct" (Jeannie Malige), this glimmer of "a certain France [...] as complicated as ancient China" (Marguerite Yourcenar), what if they move closer to us when we listen through the device Sigmund Freud discovered? It's not because the mischievous Claudine runs out on the dramatic Viennese women in a neurotic *fin de siècle* that the secrets of the "pure and impure" and the animal or floral borders of her pleasure light up in the glow of this "interior experience." Nor is it because this independent writer seduces Simone de Beauvoir herself after having condemned the feminists to a whiplashing. Colette's is an experience that the mystics practiced and which psychoanalysis restores to modern men and women. Freudian vocabulary from "depression" to "perversion" and other "sublimations" no longer offends if we take the trouble not to apply it but to deepen its meaning, as I tried to do, reading Colette in *Female Genius*.[1] Labels and clichés dissolve in proximity to Colettian desires. Today, it's the reverse of listening to her through Freud that I want to propose: how Colette's experience, as I read it in her writing, not only calls upon, deepens, displaces, and modifies psychoanalytic tools but also the conventional reception of literary genius and the very pleasures of reading.

This Jouissance of Writing [...] Named Sido

Apollinaire once described Colette as "perverse," before his preference for "mischievous,"[2] no longer hesitating to compare her provocative audacity to the tragic immodesty of the first Christians: "And so, freed from modesty, the Roman martyrs entered the arena." Perverse? Colette? Certainly, a little, or not at all. She writes whereas the perverse person tries to enjoy; that's in fact how she succeeds. She goes into action. Willy and Bertrand, with Missy en route, mark out her life. But she instantly transforms them, using some of them like an autoanalysis, by living them and meditating on them in her writing where they end up conferring its definitive form to a fictional neorealism. Duplicitous and sublime, she is at one and the same time made pearlescent with sensation, completed in the stylistic formulation/sublimation with which she becomes one. In this context, even writing functions as a kind of perverse object but one that brings about a redoubling. It displaces the subject one notch beyond the displacement brought about by a fetish in the strict sense. That is to say, it is a displacement of a displacement, a transferring of pleasure, starting with sexuality in all its sensations and, at the same time, in all its words.

Another jouissance[3] lies under *perversion's reversal into sublimation*, so that perversion itself is absorbed and, without disappearing, takes refuge in pure form. In some cases, men as well as women are capable of this and certain writers excel at it: Proust, Joyce, Nabokov, to cite only a few modern examples. Unless this kind of femininity, if specific to *another jouissance*, is the secret of all writing, its "purloined letter"?

Besides, Colette does not claim especially to be a "woman," even less a "feminist." But a feminine version of separation anxiety, which a man, identifying with his mother, might just as well share, comes to light in her through identification and rejection. Since we're "the same" (I and the mother), I don't lose "her." I enjoy her, I am this mother who enjoys, and I am then Everything through my text, sensual enough to remake the flesh of the world. In other words, the feminine relation to separation anxiety underlying perverse behavior is such that writing adds subtlety to *maternal content* (Sido, the garden, flora, and fauna, which gratify Mother Nature). In this way, writing takes possession of such content, inseparable from *the mother tongue*. The writer transports *mother and tongue* to the sublime with a knowing grace in which the cruelty of possession becomes serenity made peaceful and achieving the absolute stasis of the Eleatic philosophers.

The movements of sexual passion are there as if on the text's edge, ephemeral pre-texts to ecstasy. Sido stays—the immutable axis, character, model, archetype? Or again exquisite border between mother and language?

Designating *imaginary space itself* and moving beyond the perverse act to a clearing, where one might name pleasure, now allowed, admissible, to be shared. "Losing oneself in one's passion is less of a loss than losing one's passion," writes Saint Augustine. Lost in her passion, Colette in no way loses herself, precisely because she has never lost the fundamental passion named Sido. She balances on this sharp edge where things rise into words and where the latter in turn experience things in a reciprocal movement we identify as the dawn and secret of all humanity. Perversion? Sublimation? These terms and especially their entanglement unveiled by psychoanalysis, are only thresholds to cross in the adventurous life of the senses.

Especially to the extent that psychoanalysis, in those developments most mindful of truth, distances itself from the normativity tarnishing its fundamental notions and now considers many "perverse" behaviors as markers in the complex construction of a personality.[4] Bisexuality, to which Colette so often lays claim, is part of this. Many cures demonstrate that homosexual relations in one who does not necessarily consider herself homosexual, whether in the course of analysis in transference onto the analyst or independently of it, bring out the confusion in masculine and feminine identity, which is a common trait but most often repressed. When genital relations with a partner of the opposite sex are not accompanied by a full release of affect, the subject experiencing the lack may seek and achieve "ego orgasm"[5] or "ego promiscuity"[6] with a person of the same sex. On the one hand, this intense emotional link with more or less sublimated homosexual overtones in fact leads the conflicted subject to remember the primary identification with the infantile love object. To the extent that it is a regressive experience, the attachment brings with it the risk of the self's dissolution and confusion with the beloved object. On the other hand, if one removes these risks and the ego is strong enough (for instance beginning with strong confidence/identification with Sido!), what may emerge is a paradoxical relationship different from instinctual sublimation in Freud. Winnicott calls this amorous confidence with a homosexual or incestuous partner "ego orgasm," an experience resembling ecstasy. Certain relations, which seem to be perverse as soon as they mobilize bisexuality or incestuous impulses, bring with them this kind of ego ecstasy.

Colette herself discreetly invites us to understand in this way her bisexuality and her passage to the perverse act. In her relations with Willy, the normative genital act, accompanied by narcissistic wounds, was probably only somewhat satisfying. She also begins by strongly denying that "an amorous catastrophe, including its phases and what follows," is part of "intimacy with a woman." Besides, by divulging these erotic "half-lies" (as Colette herself did!), the woman avoids making public her "*many embarrassing secrets*, of which she herself is not very aware," buried as they are in "the very same *feminine domain, ravaged by happiness and disorder*, around which darkness thickens."[7] Whatever could have been their actual strength, the erotic pleasure obtained in these acts (disruptive relations with Willy, homosexuality with Missy, incestuous sexuality with Bertrand), proves to be—with a distance of time and with the literary future Colette was able to give them—less important than the emotional satisfaction, which these acts brought. In passing through the perverse act, the ego orgasm that characterizes them is an experience of ecstasy in which the ego finds or reestablishes direct communication with a mother/environment. Such communication may be understood as a relation of "the subjective object," recreating the interrupted maternal presence. With the *skill of illusion*, such a recreation establishes the very paradox of the "found/created" object, from now on indistinguishable from transliteration. Is Sido anything else?

A "Disingenuous Innocence": The Incestual Colette[8]

Beginning with *Claudine in Paris* (1901), and probably under Willy's influence, Colette makes reference to Krafft-Ebing, author of the famous *Psychopathia sexualis* (1886),[9] the book that was food for thought for Freud himself and remains the bible on that subject. She cites the famous alienist in an allusion to an Italian work discussing the various homosexualities hidden within boarding schools (which would be noted in *La Revue* in 1902): "This child talked to me about an amusing psychological study by one of his cohorts, which was devoted to the *Amicizie di Collegio*. This transalpine Krafft-Ebing defines them, it seems, as 'an imitation of the instinct of passion,' because, German or French, these materialists all display the most nauseating mediocre and morticolore imbecility."[10] Homosexuality was then a theme in style in literary and artistic milieus and Colette associated with many Sodomites who may have influenced the creation of the character Marcel (in *Claudine à Paris* and *La Retraite sentimentale*): Marcel Boulestin, Jean Lorrain, Edouard De Max, le marquis d'Adelsward-Fersen[11] […] She will express a complete freedom from guilt over forbidden desires in *Ces plaisirs* […] and again in *Le Pur et l'impur* (1932) : "Can you live without passion? No better than you can live with vice. And the latter comes out ahead."[12]

Along with homosexuality, a secret feminine jouissance, frenzied innocence, and solitude, with interchangeable objects, fascinates Colette. She clearly incarnates it in the character of Irène, the "hidden woman," who flees her husband less to betray him with another than to deliver herself up, wearing a mask, to the "monstrous pleasure of being alone." That is, to an autoerotic, painful, drunken state, with a variety of anonymous partners, forgetting herself, offered up in her "disingenuous innocence."[13]

But above all else, incest seems to capture the attention of Sido's daughter[14]: after *Chéri* and *Le Blé en herbe*, she practically admits it in *La Naissance du jour.* Is it necessary to recall the background for these texts, reconstructed by Bertrand de Jouvenel himself? Their relationship is scandalous, but as the main protagonist of this initiation puts it, it opens to the world. Is it because Colette assumes the role of author of this pleasure that it is also deliverance? If it is true that she is the incestuous mother, she is just as much the one who "brings into the world" Bertrand [...] and probably also herself.

Already the mother of a seven-year-old *girl*, Colette describes incest with a *boy* in her novels: she loved to praise her daughter's masculine characteristics, her sturdiness rather than her seductiveness before Maurice Goudeket's presence increasingly separated the two women.[15] Adoption/incest maybe, but incest with Bertrand may, in his eyes, constitute a satisfying revenge nevertheless. For Colette, the incestuous or incestual adventure, however, reveals the radical strangeness of the two lovers. Violating the fundamental taboo, it seems they can only assimilate their guilt as a "disturbing strangeness."

The theme of the imaginary incest between stepson and stepmother will continue to haunt Colette until *La Seconde* (1929). It endures, like a watermark beneath the main theme of the novel focused on the sublimated homosexual complicity between the two women, Fanny, the wife, and Jane, Farou the Great's mistress.

There is also Colette's article on a play about incest between a father and daughter, ending in parricide: "Paternal incest [...] really, they could have spared us that outcome –Why? Is it so grievous that a father should desire his daughter?"[16] It's not grievous that a father desires his daughter; even less if desire comes from a mother—such is the violence of human desire, its inhuman truth. The writer is expressing neither regret nor remorse. Is Colette monstrous? More likely, her uninhibited experiments uncover disturbing truths.

The Temptation of Suicide

What remains of this sadness and latent melancholy? That is to say, the well-hidden face of transgressive pleasure at the moment when it denies the drama of disidentification, of separation from the Mother. This is the face the biographical studies of Colette generally pass over in silence. The most gripping—and probably the truest—of her representations of the melancholy truth underlying her explorations of the sort found in Krafft-Ebing describes the time of a severe marital crisis—tormented by an internal "hemorrhage," one that hardens like a crab shell or like a victim who has won, having reached "the age when one no longer dies for or by anyone." Here she is twenty-nine or thirty years old—it's now 1902–1903. She also evokes suicidal temptation but by referring to the woman who succeeded in turning the death instinct aside. It's in fact Sido, the guardian goddess, appearing from the depths of her incarnation as the "other jouissance," Sido, that "purloined letter" of perverse jouissance, who made suicidal melancholy impossible. Unless, on the contrary, by "keeping her at a distance," suicide is no longer a temptation? Ambivalent Colette! At the very moment she confesses her vulnerability, death does not tempt her: "As long as Sido was alive, I never thought of a voluntary death."[17]

She almost proclaims suicide, however, in the title of another of her novels, but in reference to a man, Fred Peloux, "Peloux, the son," Léa's lover. In *La Fin de Chéri* (1926), Chéri wallows in depression and puts an end to his life, after having tried to recover the ghost of Léa, a liberated postwar young woman. Chéri had sought refuge with the "Copine," an old friend who kept Léa's memory alive in a degraded form. New habits, however, are not the only cause of this tragic dénouement. Here Colette seizes the opportunity to explore a melancholy version of memory by putting in play a hero who is too accepting of a past that kills. In counterpoint to the childlike enthusiasm of the invigorating *La Maison de Claudine*, however, the author's unconscious motivation, which animates *La Fin de Chéri*, is perhaps more complex.

Beyond avenging a cheating husband, Colette's pen also aims at the young man morbidly attached to a false mother, a man thrown outside time and consequently destined to die. But *La Fin de Chéri*, this novel so intent on getting even, is not so much concerned with the real figure of the incestuous son. At this time, her relationship with Bertrand is over and Maurice Goudeket has already entered the writer's life. In fact, considering her many affirmations of a virile identification, one can see a masculine version of Colette in the character Chéri. The narrator projects herself onto Léa and also onto Fred through her relation to the former. This complementary movement, which she outlines in exploring the perverse connection, has her confront her phallic aspirations and their inevitable failure in another way.

Yes, she will be the man who fully satisfies her mother, but which man? The father, an invalid and failed writer in the guise of an amorous hero? The older brother Achille Robineau-Duclos, a valuable doctor but so attached to the mother that he dies a year after Sido's death? The younger brother Léo, the "sylph," a charming failed musician, so tortured by childhood memories that he can share them only with his sister? He accepted only "a mute role, that of 'the idiot son.'"[18] If it is probable that Colette was eager to "kill the son symbolically"[19] in writing *La Fin de Chéri*, it is also likely that *she herself is the son* in fantasy. Four years pass between *La Maison de Claudine* and *La Fin de Chéri* (1926). Through writing, she executes the "analysis" of the incestuous and incestual connection without omitting any of this adventure's reversible roles and it leads to the reversal of the transgressive exaltation, its melancholic-suicidal lining. Colette can in this way construct *La Naissance du jour* (1928) and *Sido* (1929) in her recovered calm. Pure or impure, what remains? Who am I if I am neither Léa nor Chéri ? The torrent that is "Sido."

Beyond the seductive power of her works, Colette's complicity with various aspects of perversion and her experience of them offers up a message with psychoanalytic resonance. A suicidal depressivity exists, following from the virile identification (I am Chéri) of a woman in her incestuous desire for the mother, she seems to say with *La Fin de Chéri*. Colette initiates the loss of this fantasy, without abandoning her attachment to the maternal object or her phallic aspiration to dominate the other, in the course of an experience both sexual and writerly. Her writing can from now on continue to explore this economy while detaching itself from the Oedipal triangle and its substitutes, once her self-analysis achieves an abreaction via writing, as we have seen: she is then better able to position herself in the flesh of the world.

A Melancholy Choked Back, or a Drop of Blood from the Experience of Time

Depressivity certainly awaits many heroines and has darkened many expressions of the author's own itinerary, because a woman, "a surprising animal, part poet, part starling, part model lawyer"[20], often skirts melancholy, without giving in to it completely, according to Colette. Examples include Minne ("Her inactive melancholy amuses itself") who also foils Maugis's (Willy's) "real melancholy"[21]; Renée Néré in *La Vagabonde*, who "attracts" and retains "those bent on the life of a recluse or vagabond—the melancholy, the solitary, like her"[22]; or even Claudine evoking love "and all of its incurable and precious melancholy" with Annie.[23] All of them are reflections of the little girl who was never really a child: "I grew up, but I was never little. I never changed [...]."[24]

Colette outlines her particular position, which is, I repeat, psychic behavior *and* a writing style, through these fictional characters, however. Colette the writer forges her art not to deepen this unhappiness nor to uncover or go beyond it. The Nordic, English, or Slavic novel, or therapy might do so. But no, her heroines up to Julie de Carneilhan,[25] for instance, know how to create a mask of indifference over the sadness they feel. Colette prefers to repress unhappiness, to kill the killer who is in despair in order to build on its tomb. "I cry as much, as sadly as a man. But you conquer yourself provided you really want to [...]."[26] You establish a way of life, inseparable from a writing style, underpinned by the certainty of never experiencing any kind of lack at all, of always containing lost time and any loss to come. There is no mourning: it's possible to possess everything in the style of remembering via the senses. "*I do without what I miss* [...]. you are never completely without something that you know well because you in fact possessed it."[27] The experience of depression, written in *La Fin de Chéri*, also passes through a denial, choked back as well. Colette feels a strong repulsion for sickness and old age and ends up thinking that sadness does not deserve her attention, "I have a very clear memory of my pets caring less for me when I was suffering from a lover's betrayal. They caught the scent of a major decline, of pain in me."[28]

An unshakeable faith in the psychic strength of women is the result of these two intersecting movements—on the one hand, the exploration of a suicidal tendency with *La Fin de Chéri*, and on the other, the repudiation of this sickening decline. A woman doesn't die of unhappiness and knows how to go beyond this intrinsic weakness rendering her so vulnerable to love. Colette fears this weakness, which she calls "mediocrity," to the point where she kills it in the bud, "How many women have known this withdrawal into self, this patient turning inward, which follows outraged tears? I'll give them credit, at the same time flattering myself: it is only in sadness that a woman can go beyond her mediocrity." She speaks of her skepticism awakened by the clichés of the betrayed woman, for instance, these so-called fatal, unhappy affairs, and to what extent the "very solid creature" is "difficult to kill." She even affirms that it is in "suffering and acting a part" that "she [a woman] exerts herself and becomes flexible, as in a daily exercise full of risks [...] Because she constantly skirts the temptation that is most poignant, sweet, and adorned with attractions: that of avenging herself."[29]

Colette emphasizes the difficulty, even impossibility, represented by the loss of one's mother, given that the "mediocrity" she describes is in fact a fundamental feminine depressivity. The proof is that the woman desperately, to no avail, seeks her mother in a lover/husband—who, according to Sido, is "not even a relative." Thus, the heterosexual couple is by definition an uncertain relationship and bound to fail. An imaginary solution exists: never separate from this impossible loss (the Mother), but carry her within like a hidden jewel, an invisible sadness, that you bury like a secret pleasure.

Mastery of the separation's pain in its different phases does become stronger and more refined with time, but it is still burning with intensity in 1908 when *Les Vrilles de la vigne* appears, "You deepen the spot of the recent wound with brute desire, without succeeding in releasing the living, fresh drop of blood—you struggle over a half-dry scar, missing, I swear, the strong, sharp burning!" Sure of herself and already triumphant in having overcome this pain, *La Vagabonde* (1910) can retort, "And he can ask me with the tone of a master, 'Where are you going?'" "Female I was, and female I still am, to suffer and enjoy it."[30] *Ces plaisirs* [...] (1932) on their part reveal a weary, clever woman, "The veiled face of a sensitive woman who knows how to dissemble, to be subtle, suits the opening of this book and its sad words concerning pleasure."[31] Colette will toss this crushing remark to Don Juan-Damien who wonders what women could have given him in the end, "What they gave you? Well, their pain, I think. Not a bad gift, I'd say!"[32]

She preserves serenity against endemic sadness, thanks to that torrent of exaltation named "Sido." The petrification of sadness takes refuge in this serenity, like a precious treasure, which is the silent silver lining of radiant joy, and in the end, you forget your distress. The memory of the native land absorbs sad love affairs and even possesses the magic of transforming them: "A woman claims as many native lands as she has happy love affairs. She is reborn everywhere she has found a cure for the sadness of loving."[33] One experience alone--it, too, part of this "torrent" and so vital--continues to feed itself with sadness and at times exalts it: its writing, "perilous and deceptive,"[34] "the scar that fascinates [...]."

A contrapuntal ode to joy can finally emerge, while the sacred Sido makes herself heard as a cult of plants or animals, even if human happiness is really deceptive. A certain kind of happiness exists, beyond our passing setbacks and thanks to the exquisite perversity in which animals excel, accompanied, naturally, by Colette and Sido. All the rest is literature.

And yet, the evidence stares you in the face: the cosmic Sido was the beloved [...] of the Captain. To love Sido, in the sense of enjoying, transubstantiating, writing her, implies replacing Captain Colette. Consider this hypothesis: the true "purloined letter" of jouissance, according to Colette the Great, is—with and hidden behind Sido—none other than Jules-Joseph Colette. The magic *object* of writing is called "Sido," but the *subject* of the writing we read, comment on, and admire is actually, precisely, the paternal patronym. The *other jouissance* hides a black spot. Sadness, lurking in the very exaltation of writing, has remained tied to the father whose name retains his hidden trace.

From Sadness as "Exercise" to the Repair of the Amputated Father

The charming and somewhat ridiculous papa of Claudine the school girl is an expert in malacology, more attached to gastropods than to his daughter. It's not surprising then to learn that her husband Renaud will have as his principal mission to replace this fantasy father and that his position is that of a "paternal lover."[35] To the young woman's eyes, this ambiguous character is also "more feminine than virile. He loves me—that's clear—and more than anything, thank God, I love him—that too is clear. But he is so much more a woman than I am! How much more simple I feel, more brutal [...] more somber, more passionate [...]"[36] Whatever the case, Claudine submits to him like a "battered child."

When Captain Colette dies, September 17, 1905, Sido writes to her oldest daughter, Juliette, the child of her first marriage, "I will not try to describe the depth of my sadness to you."[37] Colette, expert at hardening herself, does not betray the slightest emotion that day and her only memory of the funeral will be that of a "cheerful burial."[38] In this same year, she and Willy divide their possessions.

The Captain's resurrection in his daughter's work will be slow, following the preparation of the terrain for Sido's gradual appearance. An exception appears in the text "Un zouave," published in installments in *Le Matin* on May 27 and June 10, 1915.[39] The strong portrait and warm filial emotion precedes the as yet hesitant sketch of maternal traits sprinkled here and there,[40] which will not crystallize until *La Maison de Claudine* (1922). The First World War, which mobilizes Colette as a journalist, at that time the young wife of Henry de Jouvenel, clearly contributes to this crystallization of the Captain's features into a war hero. The "soldier in love with combat had left his whole left leg, cut above the thigh, in Italy in 1859 at Melegnano."[41]

The image of the amputated father, all the sadder because of its discretion, appears in *La Maison de Claudine*: "I hear the rhythm rocking my entire youth grow fainter--two canes and a single foot."[42] In *Sido*, Colette reveals a silent suffering in the Captain, which only the daughter detects. This remains unthinkable [...] for her mother. But most significant, Colette confesses to herself this poignant expression of a denied pain, "It's never too late, given that I have penetrated what my youth had hidden from me: my brilliant, joyful father nursed a deep sadness, that of the amputee."[43]

If, for the unconscious, amputation is a brutal symbol of castration, the feminine first name serving as the family name nonetheless contributes to his feminization. A man called Colette, obedient to the wife he loves, and who, on top of that, one-legged, is certainly enough to shatter the phallic image of the father who incarnates interdiction and the law, without Doctor Freud getting involved! One no longer wonders why Minet-Chéri, as if to spice up and ward off these traits, falls in love with the likes of the perverse Willy and is so intrigued by *Psychopathia sexualis* [...].

Her father's physical weakness is, however, not the most painful thing for the daughter. At least she succeeds in compensating for this paternal handicap by worshiping his powerful musculature whose "feline force"[44] (is he Colette's first "cat man"?) is all the more impressive because it manifests itself in the hand and in anger, which together take aim at paper, the writer's privileged tool. The "little one" was not unaware of this: "It didn't escape me that his white hand crumpled, rolled, and destroyed paper with explosive fury, as my hands did, especially from the time that my thumb stuck out like his. And then his anger [...] I won't talk about my anger, which comes from him." The angry strength and Mediterranean fury of Colette the father naturally arouses Sido's fascination, at the same time disapproving: "Italian! [...] The man with a knife!",[45] while her daughter admires the athletic elegance of this virility, whose fine skin she looks for in all of her lovers and husbands.

Incestual harmony with her father accumulates with the pages, putting forward the image of a seductive, women-loving man who is a good singer and rakish in a charming way. But aside from Sido, it's his own daughter who Colette-the-father keeps close to his heart, despite any other real or imaginary feminine conquest. Is her retrospective surprise a pretense when she discovers his attachment? "But I see that his letters (I learn this twenty years after his death) are full of my name, of the 'little one's' pain [...]"[46] We remember this when we see her tenderly submitting to the "paternal vice" of Willy, that great lover of "young things."

Captain Colette, poet, citizen, and Sido's ardent lover, is the perfect antithesis of the cosmic woman. A primary example, his "deplorable sociability. drew him to politics."[47] The Zouave's daughter's disapproval will only increase once she becomes the Baroness de Jouvenel—Sido will learn a thing or two about that! But above all, the Captain does not understand nature. He stubbornly insists on Sunday picnics, while Sido and his children, who are uncivilized, don't care much for that, immersed night and day in grass, woods, and flowers!

That man who passes over his military exploits in silence[48] is passionate about everything having to do with writing. He is vociferous in expressing his passion for newspapers and books, collects pens and wax seals, for all of which his daughter too develops a real passion, associating the invalid with his library from the time of *La Maison de Claudine*. After his death, Colette unveils her father's failure only in the writing of *Sido* where she deals with her painful discovery of a writer without works: "I can still see on one of the highest shelves of the library a series of volumes bound in black fabric. The rigid binding with the well-glued colored paper attested to my father's manual dexterity [...]. Two, three, five hundred pages per volume; beautiful, creamy, laid paper or thick 'schoolboy' sheets, carefully cut, hundreds and hundreds of white pages [...]. An imaginary oeuvre, mirage of a writer's career."[49] Without self-pity or laughter, she accepts her father's lack of power with an understanding that is completely [...] fraternal, yes, showing solidarity with his pain and quickly moving on—not without making known the name of the would-be writer in the pantheon of letters.

It's not a shocked woman (in reality secretly overjoyed) who contemplates the Captain's virgin pages. Sido, on the one hand, can take on a kind of vengeful attitude and gently make fun of him, covering her own work, jars of preserves, with her husband's useless sheets [...] Colette, the daughter, on the contrary, anchors in them her determination to persevere in the effort to write in Willy's studio. It's a question of fulfilling the Captain's dedication, the work that he had only planned as a homage to Sido and of which he was able to write only a few lines: "I dared to cover over with my huge round letters the invisible cursive of which only one person in the world perceived the luminous watermark, which extended into glory the only page completed and signed with love, the dedication page: 'For my beloved soul-mate,/ her faithful husband/ Jules-Joseph Colette.' "[50]

It will be a brilliant accomplishment, but not without the daughter's continuing to feel deep within the amputee's anguish and fear of never succeeding. Until her death, Colette will be haunted by the specter of the Captain, which inflicts on her, on the one hand, the "muscular" need to write—"I run into you, I feel your presence"— and, on the other, the threat of impotence with the fear of being like him. The discovery of the blank pages left by the Captain was so overwhelming that one can only imagine the trauma and compensatory, restorative decision, which followed it. Yet, extensive signs must have let Colette-the-daughter guess the weakness of the would-be-writer-Colette-the father. Along with his unconsciously bequeathing her in his will that she accomplish precisely *that.*

Her? Really? The little 10-year-old daughter who was his primary, uncompromising literary critic? In fact, the Captain reserved for her the reading of his "oratory prose, or of an ode, easy verses, sumptuous in their rhythm, their rhyme, sonorous as a storm in the mountains." And he awaits her judgment confidently, when, insolent youth, Colette-the daughter, bluntly cuts off discussion and issues the verdict: "Always too many adjectives."[51] Colette-the-father, turns red with anger, excoriating the future great Colette, "the vermin, the egotistical flea that I was." Oedipal though it is, and this is an inverted Oedipal complex (since the daughter "murders" her father's writing, like a son), the scene is nevertheless formative. The father's theatrical love for his daughter and his both real and apparent anger, prepare, at one and the same time, guilt towards the amputee, the failed writer, and the little girl's embarking on her destiny as a writer. The discovery of his blank portfolio later on will encourage this path. Remember above all the daughter/father complicity, which Sido doesn't suspect, "She thought he was carefree, because he sang. But, I, who whistle the instant I'm sad [...] I wish she would have understood that there is nothing as offensive as pity."

"He Reappears [...]"

Colette explicitly traces her career as a writer back to the captain, before she reunites Maman and Papa to recognize her debt to both, though different in each case. She implies that their first crossing of swords over the question of style was the beginning of the real transmission of the "lyrical" talent for which Willy reproached her so much. She finds a way to preserve it, however, by refining it to the extreme, to the point where she achieves a glory forever her own, "He wanted to reappear and live again, when I began to write with a great deal of uncertainty."

After some revealing hesitations in her drafts, Colette makes clear that she owes her nickname Bel-Gazou (provençal? Persian? she wonders, dreaming), which she transfers to her own daughter: a solemn sacred rite, if ever there was one, of the Captain as the patriarch of the whole family line. The two proper names Colette creates, her pen name and the affectionate pet name given to her daughter, are signifiers owing to father Colette. Furthermore, it is only after a triple mention of the name Colette to designate the father and daughter in *La Maison de Claudine* in 1923[52] that the writer definitively adopts her family name as her pen name, abandoning Colette Willy and Colette de Jouvenel.

In reality and more slyly, the motive which aroused this rivalry and ends up with "paternal lyricism" metamorphosing into the jewel of French literature signed "Colette," is none other than jealousy. She thinks the demon of "jealousy, which made me so difficult to deal with in the past"[53] along with the outbursts of anger, come from Colette-the-father. The father's jealousy, or rather the daughter's, concerning the father *and* mother? This man who in the past took all the risks of battle, now mutilated, remained at Sido's side.

We can believe Colette when she recreates her predecessors. In fact, such an extreme love for Maman can only arouse the intense desire of the girl/boy to conquer this definitive object of paternal love in turn, with jealousy. This object so much desired very visibly retained her individual character. All the more so in that Sido does not fail to point out her superiority to the Captain. Doesn't she possess her children, while he simply wanted to be like them—a child of his wife's? And Sido even goes so far as to disown this "great love," which, however, honors her, since she sees in it the reason for the Captain's failure, this poor soul who preferred to love a woman instead of creating a work. This is certainly a mistake to avoid [...] At least that is how the daughter deciphers it. From then on, it remains for her to love differently than the Zouave, to write Sido as Monsieur Colette was not able to do. Such a project leads to the blooming of a great [...] Colette.

Notes

1 Julia Kristeva, "*Colette*," in *Female Genius: Life, Madness, Words—Hannah Arendt, Melanie Klein, Colette*, vol. 3, trans. Jane Marie Todd (New York: Columbia University Press, 2004).

2 Guillaume Apollinaire, "Sur la littérature féminine," in *Œuvres Complètes*, vol. II, ed. Claude Pichois (Paris: Gallimard, 1991), p. 923.

3 Jacques Lacan insists on the difference between *pleasure* and *jouissance*, and adds to *phallic jouissance* "*another jouissance*," which the woman experiences but is not able to name or know and which puts her in a relation with the Other resulting in a structural duplicity. See Kristeva (2004), 222–223.

4 Joyce McDougall makes a case, in carefully attending to the perverse, for a recognition of these neosexualities. See "De la douleur psychotique et du psychosoma" in *Plaidoyer pour une certaine anormalité* (Paris: Gallimard, 1978), pp. 184–202 and "Déviation sexuelle et survie psychique" in *Éros aux mille visages* (Paris: Gallimard, 1996), pp. 250–268.

5 This is D. W. Winnicott's term in "The Capacity to be Alone," in *Collected Papers: Through Paediatrics to Psychoanalysis* (London: Tavistock, 1958), p. 34.
6 See Masud Khan, "Orgasme du moi dans l'amour bisexual," in *Figures de la perversion* (Paris: Gallimard, 1979), p. 239.
7 Colette, *La Naissance du jour*, in *Œuvres*, vol. III, ed. Claude Pichois(Paris: Gallimard, 1991), pp. 315–316. (All translations of Colette in this essay are my own. CMB.)
8 One uses the term "incestuous" to refer to incest (sexual relations between relatives) and one reserves "incestual" for what carries the trace of incest in the psychic lives of individuals or families—with or without progression to the genital act, or in transgressing generational difference, for instance, between partners taking on parental roles.
9 His *Médecine légale des aliénés* is translated into French in 1900. Richard von Krafft-Ebing, *Médecine légale des aliénés* (Paris: Doin / Larose, 1900).
10 Colette, *Claudine à Paris*, in *Œuvres*, vol. I, ed. Claude Pichois (Paris: Gallimard, 1984), p. 301. (Pichois explains Colette's use of "morticolore" as a contraction of "morticole" [often an incompetent doctor] and "incolore" [colorless] ; I am providing some of the information in these notes. CMB).
11 Colette, Notice, *Le Pur et l'Impur*, in *Œuvres*, vol. III (1991), p. 1503.
12 Colette, *Le Pur et l'Impur*, in *Œuvres*, vol. III (1991), p. 652.
13 Colette, *La Femme cachéé*, in *Œuvres*, vol. III (1991), p. 6.
14 See Jeanine Malige, *Colette, qui êtes-vous?* (Lyon: La Manufacture, 1987).
15 Claude Pichois, Préface, in Colette, *Oeuvres*, vol. II (1986), p. L.
16 Colette, Notes, *Bella Vista*, in *Œuvres*, vol. III (1991), pp. 1901–1902.
17 Colette, *Mes apprentissages*, in *Œuvres*, vol. III (1991), p. 1052.
18 Colette, *Le Pur et l'Impur, Œuvres*, vol. III (1991), p. 534.
19 As Claude Pichois notes, Préface, in Colette, *Œuvres*, vol. II, p. L.
20 Colette, "Les joyaux menacés," in *Le Voyage égoïste*, in *Œuvres*, vol. II (1986), p. 1135.
21 Colette, "Les joyaux menacés," p. 792.
22 Colette, *La Vagabonde*, in *Œuvres*, vol. I (1984), p. 1107.
23 Colette, *La Retraite sentimentale*, in *Oeuvres*, vol. I, (1984), pp. 863–864.
24 Colette, "Le miroir, " in *Les Vrilles de la vigne*, in *Œuvres*, vol. I, (1984), p. 1032.
25 Colette, *Julie de Carneilhan*, in *Colette*, vol. III, ed. Françoise Burgaud (Paris: Bouquins, 2004), p. 30: "a sadness, the depths into which she forbade herself to descend."
26 Colette, *Mes apprentissages*, in *Œuvres*, vol. III (1991), p. 1000.
27 Colette, *Le Pur et l'Impur, Œuvres*, vol. III (1991), p. 565; my italics (JK).
28 Colette, *La Naissance du jour, Œuvres*, vol. III (1991), pp. 286–287.
29 Colette, *La Vagabonde, Œuvres*, vol. I, p. 1087.
30 Colette, *La Vagabonde*, p. 1184.
31 *Le Pur et l'Impur, Œuvres*, vol. III (1991), p. 566.
32 Colette, *Le Pur et l'Impur*, p. 581.
33 Colette, *La Naissance du jour, Œuvres*, vol. III (1991), p. 282.
34 Colette, *La Vagabonde, Œuvres*, vol. I (1984), p. 1074.
35 Colette, *Claudine en ménage, Œuvres*, vol. I (1984), p. 411.
36 Colette, *Claudine en ménage*, p. 414.
37 Claude Pichois, Préface, in Colette, *Œuvres*, vol. I, p. LXXXIV.
38 Colette, "Un zouave," in *Les Heures longues, Œuvres*, vol. II (1986), p. 524 and "Le rire," in *La Maison de Claudine, Œuvres*, vol. II (1986), , pp. 1049–1051.
39 Colette, "Un zouave," pp. 521–524.

40 J. Kristeva, *Colette*, "Qui est Sido?," 175–181.
41 Colette, "Un zouave," in *Les Heures longues*, *Œuvres*, vol. II, p. 524.
42 Colette, *La Maison de Claudine*, p. 976.
43 Colette, *La Maison de Claudine*, p. 524. [sic] The quotation is from Colette, "Le Capitaine," in *Sido* in *Oeuvres*, vol. III. (CB)
44 Colette, *La Maison de Claudine*, p. 518. [sic] The quotation is from Colette, "Le Capitaine," in *Sido* in *Oeuvres*, vol. III. (CB)
45 Colette, *La Maison de Claudine*, p. 519. [sic] The quotation is from Colette, "Le Capitaine," in *Sido* in *Oeuvres*, vol. III. (CB)
46 Colette, *La Maison de Claudine*, p. 521. [sic] The quotation is from Colette, "Le Capitaine," in *Sido*, in *Œuvres*, vol. III, p. 521. (CB)
47 Colette, *La Maison de Claudine*, p. 512. [sic] This quotation is from the same page as the previous one, p. 521, of Colette, "Le Capitaine," in *Sido*, in *Œuvres*, vol. III. (CB)
48 Colette, *La Maison de Claudine*, p. 521. "Strange silence for a man who spoke freely: he didn't tell stories about his military heroism." This quotation is from the same page as the two previous, p. 521, of Colette, "Le Capitaine," in *Sido*, in *Œuvres*, vol. III. (CB)
49 "Le Capitaine," pp. 531–532.
50 "Le Capitaine," p. 532.
51 "Le Capitaine," p. 517.
52 Colette, *La Maison de Claudine*, pp. 997, 1049, and 1073.
53 Colette, *La Naissance du jour*, p. 364.

BIBLIOGRAPHY

Ahmed, Sara. *Queer Phenomenology: Orientations, Objects, Others.* Durham, NC: Duke University Press, 2006.

Anderson, John. Review of Westmoreland's *Colette*. "*Colette*: Literary history with a modern flavor." *The Wall Street Journal*, September 21, 2018, A11. http://pitt.idm.oclc.org/login?url=https://www.proquest.com/newspapers/life-amp-arts-film-review-colette-literary/docview/2109826668/se-2?accountid=14709.

Beauvoir, Simone de. "The Married Woman." In *The Second Sex*. Translated by Constance Borde and Sheila Malovany-Chevallier, 439–524. New York: Vintage, 2011.

Bellour, Raymond. "To Analyze, to Segment." *Quarterly Review of Film Studies* 1, no. 3 (August 1976): 331–353.

Best, Stephen and Sharon Marcus. "Surface Reading: An Introduction." *Representations* 108, no. 1 (2009): 1–21. https://doi.org/10.1525/rep.2009.108.1.1.

Birgy, Philippe and Aurélie Guillain. Introduction to "Modernism and the Obscene." *Miranda* 21 (2020). https://doi.org/10.4000/miranda.27682.

Borges, Jorge Luis. "Borges and I." In *Collected Fictions*, Translated by Andrew Hurley, 324. London: Penguin, 1999.

Bové, Carol Mastrangelo. *Language and Politics in Julia Kristeva: Literature, Art, Therapy.* Albany, NY: SUNY Press, 2006.

———"The Thimble and the Needle: Translating *La Maison de Claudine*." *Palimpsestes* 24 (2012): 131–147.

———"Translating Colette: Bisexuality and Modernism in *La Maison de Claudine*." In *Translation and Literary Studies: Homage to Marilyn Gaddis Rose*. Edited by Marella Feltrin-Morris, Deborah Folaron, and Maria Costanza Guzman, 16–24. New York: Routledge, 2016.

———*Kristeva in America: Re-Imagining the Exceptional.* New York: Palgrave, 2020.

———"Modernist Trajectories in Time: Kristeva's *The Enchanted Clock*." In *Understanding Modernism: Understanding Kristeva*. Edited by Maria Margaroni, 75–91. London: Bloomsbury, 2022.

Bowen, Peter. "Who's Who in *Colette*." On the Bleeker Street site for Westmoreland's film *Gigi*. n.d., ca. 2018. https://bleeckerstreetmedia.com/editorial/whos-who-in-colette.

Caldwell, Christopher. "Is This the End of French Intellectual Life?" *The New York Times* (Mar. 5, 2021). https://www.nytimes.com/2021/03/05/opinion/french-intellectual-life-america.html?searchResultPosition=6.

Clark, Nick. "Gigi: How a West London Theatre Is Putting the Darkness Back into a Play Best Known as a Sunny Musical." *Independent* (October 17, 2015). https://www.independent.co.uk/arts-entertainment/theatre-dance/news/gigi-how-a-west-london-theatre-is-putting-the-darkness-back-into-a-play-best-known-as-a-sunny-musical-a6698421.html.

Cohen, Susan. "An Onomastic Double Bind: Colette's Gigi and the Politics of Naming." *PMLA* 100, no. 5 (October 1985): 93–809.

Colette. *Break of Day*. Translated by Enid McLeod. New York: Farrar, Straus & Giroud, 1979.

———*La Maison de Claudine*. Edited by Claude Pichois, 965–1084. Vol. II of *Œuvres*. Paris: Gallimard, 1986.

———*Le Pur et l'impur*. Edited by Claude Pichois, 551–653. Vol. III of *Œuvres*. Paris: Gallimard, 1991.

———*Gigi, Julie De Carneilan, and Other Acquaintances: Three Short Novels*. Translated by Roger Senhouse & Patrick Leigh Fermor. New York: Farrar, Straus & Giroud, 2001.

———*Gigi*. Edited by Claude Pichois et al., 433–476. Vol. IV of *Œuvres*. Paris: Gallimard, 2001.

———*My Mother's House and Sido*. Translated by Una Vincenzo Troubridge & Enid McLeod. New York: Farrar, Straus & Giroud, 2002.

———*Claudine's House*. Translated by Andrew Brown. London: Hesperus, 2006.

———*Chéri and The End of Chéri*. Translated by Rachel Careau. New York: W.W. Norton & Co., 2022.

Colette, dir. Wash Westmoreland. Film script by Wash Westmoreland and Richard Glatzer. Colette Film Holdings, Ltd, 2017. https://script-pdf.s3-us-west-2.amazonaws.com/colette-script-pdf.pdf.

Colette, dir. Wash Westmoreland. 2018; Santa Monica, CA: Lionsgate Home Entertainment, 2019. DVD.

Corner, Lewis. "*Colette* director Wash Westmoreland on 'the invisible revolution' in His Queer Period Drama." *Gay Times* (December 30, 2018). https://www.gaytimes.co.uk/culture/colette-wash-westmoreland-interview/.

Degler, Carl. "The Case of the Origin of the Incest Taboo." In *In Search of Human Nature: The Decline and Revival of Darwinism in American Social Thought*, 245–269. London: Oxford University Press, 1992. https://ebookcentral.proquest.com/lib/pitt-ebooks/reader.action?docID=3051870&ppg=258.

Di Cecco, Daniela, ed. *Girls in French and Francophone Literature and Film*. Leiden, The Netherlands: Brill/Rodopi, 2015.

Doubrovsky, Serge. *Writing and Fantasy in Proust: La Place de la Madeleine*. Translated by Carol Mastrangelo Bové and Paul Bové. Lincoln and London: University of Nebraska Press, 1986.

Engelking, Tama L. "Reading the Romance with Colette in 'La Lune de pluie.'" *Modern Language Studies* 47, no. 1 (summer 2017): 26–45. https://engagedscholarship.csuohio.edu/clmlang_facpub/142/.

———"Crossing Borders with Colette's *Gigi*." *The French Review* 93, no. 3 (2020): 102–115. https://works.bepress.com/tama_engelking/32/.

Epstein, Robert, S. D. Bock, M. J. Drew et al. "Infantilization cross the Lifespan: A Large-Scale Internet Study Suggests That Emotional Abuse Is Especially Damaging." *Motivation and Emotion* 47 (2023): 137–163. https://doi.org/10.1007/s11031-022-09989-4.

Ferrari, Alain. "Mon dernier voyage terrestre: Colette et le cinéma." In L'Herne: *Colette*. Edited by Gérard Bonal & Frédéric Maget, 161–169. Paris: L'Herne, 2011.

Flieger, Jerry Aline. *Colette and the Fantom Subject of Autobiography*. Ithaca: Cornell University Press, 1992.

Gigi, dir. Vincente Minnelli. 1958; Los Angeles County, CA: Studio Distribution Services, 2010. DVD.

Hansen, Ellis. "The Future's Eve: Reparative Reading after Sedgwick." *South Atlantic Quarterly* 110, no. 1 (2011): 101–119. https://read.dukeupress.edu/south-atlantic-quarterly/article-abstract/110/1/101/3506/The-Future-s-Eve-Reparative-Reading-after-Sedgwick?redirectedFrom=fulltext.

Harvey, Stephen. "Darkening Beauty: On Some Films of Vincente Minnelli." *MoMA* 2, no. 2 (Autumn, 1989): 14–16. https://www.jstor.org/stable/4381091.

Ibtisaam. "*Colette*: A Film Without Jouissance." *Medium* (a blog), Oct. 20, 2018. https://medium.com/@ibtisaamahmed/colette-a-film-without-jouissance-b7456ad730eb.

James, Robin. "From Receptivity to Transformation: On the Intersection of Race, Gender, and the Aesthetic in Contemporary Continental Philosophy." In *Convergences: Black Feminism and Continental Philosophy*. Edited by Kathryn Gines, Donna-Dale Marcano & Maria Davidson, 135–156. Albany, NY: SUNY Press, 2010. https://philarchive.org/rec/JAMFRT.

Johnson, Albert. "The Films of Vincente Minnelli: Part II." *Film Quarterly* 12, no. 3 (Spring, 1959): 39.

Judy, Ronald A. *Sentient Flesh: Thinking in Disorder, Poiesis in Black*. Durham, NC: Duke University Press, 2020. https://doi.org/10.1215/9781478012559.

Keough, Peter. Review of Westmoreland's *Colette*. *The Boston Globe*, September 26, 2018. https://www.bostonglobe.com/arts/2018/09/26/keira-knightley-takes-writer-pen-colette/1sUkv8wotVjVnWBo9NLqiL/story.html.

Kristeva, Julia. *Powers of Horror*, Translated by Leon Roudiez. New York: Columbia University Press, 1982.

———"Stabat Mater." In *Tales of Love*. Translated by Leon Roudiez, 234–263. New York: Columbia University Press, 1987.

———*Time and Sense*. Translated by Ross Guberman. New York: Columbia University Press, 1996.

———*Intimate Revolt*. Translated by Jeanine Herman. New York: Columbia University Press, 2002.

———*Colette* Vol. 3. *Female Genius: Life, Madness, Words—Hannah Arendt, Melanie Klein, Colette*, Translated by Jane Marie Todd. New York: Columbia University Press, 2004.

———"Ni Dépression ni perversion: éclosion." In *l'Herne Colette*. Edited by Gérard Bonal and Frédéric Maget, 19–28. Paris: L'Herne, 2011.

———"Ni Dépression ni perversion: l'éclosion Colette." In *Pulsions du temps*. 305–329. Paris: Fayard, 2013.

Ladenson, Elizabeth. "Colette aux Etats-Unis." *Cahiers Colette* 19 (1997): 217–228.

Laplanche, Jean and Jean-Bertrand Pontalis. *The Language of Psychoanalysis*. Translated by Donald Nicholson-Smith. New York: Norton, 1973.

Lapointe, Michael. "The Brilliance of Colette: A Writer, who Prized the Body Over the Mind." *The New Yorker* (November 15, 2022). https://www.newyorker.com/books/under-review/the-brilliance-of-colette-a-novelist-who-prized-the-body-over-the-mind.

Lawson, Richard. Review of Westmoreland's *Colette*. *Vanity Fair*, January 21, 2018. https://www.vanityfair.com/hollywood/2018/01/colette-lizzie-borden-movie-reviews-keira-knightley-chloe-sevigny.

Leininger, Alex. "*Colette* Upends the Biopic's Stodgy Maleness." *PopMatters*, October 17, 2018. https://www.popmatters.com/colette-upends-the-biopics-stodgy-maleness-2612885103.html.

Lessing, Doris. Foreword to *Claudine's House*. Translated by Andrew Brown, vii–x. London: Hesperus Press, 2005.

Levy, Emanuel. "Gigi (1958): Minnelli Oscar-Winning Musical." *Cinema 24/7* (July 17, 2006). https://emanuellevy.com/review/gigi-1958-4/.

Lockett, Abby. "From Déesse to Idée: The Woman-Child in French New Wave Film." Capstone Research, The University of Texas at Austin, 2015. https://www.academia.edu/29009946/From_D%C3%A9esse_to_Id%C3%A9e_The_Woman_child_in_French_New_Wave_Film.

Lucey, Michael. *Never Say I: Sexuality and the First Person in Colette, Gide, and Proust*. Durham, NC: Duke, 2006. Kindle.

Lukács, György. *The Theory of the Novel*. Translated by Anna Bostak. Cambridge, MA: MIT Press, 1974.

Margaroni, Maria. 2007. "Recent Work on and by Julia Kristeva: Toward a Psychoanalytic Social." *Signs* 32, no. 3 (Spring 2007): 793–808.

McKafee, Noëlle. "Abject Strangers: Toward an Ethics of Respect." In *Ethics, Politics, and Difference in Julia Kristeva's Writing*. Edited by Kelly Oliver, 116–134. New York & London: Routledge, 1993.

Merleau-Ponty, Maurice. *The Visible and the Invisible*. Translated by Alphonso Lingis. Evanston Ill: Northwestern University Press, 1968.

Michallon, Clémance. "Why *Colette* Will Open the Door to More Queer Period Dramas." *The Independent* (January 12, 2019). https://www.independent.co.uk/arts-entertainment/films/features/colette-keira-knightley-bisexual-dominic-west-movie-queer-period-drama-a8718286.html.

Michineau, Stéphanie. "L'Autofiction dans l'œuvre de Colette." *Semat: An International Journal* 1, no. 1 (2013): 1–9. https://www.naturalspublishing.com/files/published/96487z73y4td8l.pdf.

Mulvey, Laura. "Visual Pleasure and Narrative Cinema." *Screen* 16, no. 3 (Autumn 1975): 6–18.

Oxford English Dictionary. s.v. "fairy (n.), sense 4.c," December 2023. https://doi.org/10.1093/OED/2781028924.

Parker, Seymour. "The Precultural Basis of the Incest Taboo: Toward a Biosocial Theory." *American Anthropologist* 78, no. 2 (June 1976): 285–305. https://www.jstor.org/stable/675233.

Proust, Marcel. *Le Côté de Guermantes*. Edited by Jean-Yves Tadié. Vol. II of *À la recherche du temps perdu*. Paris: Gallimard, 1954.

Racamier, Paul-Claude. *L'inceste et l'incestuel*. Paris: Dunod, 2021.

Robcis, Camille. "Lévi-Strauss's Structuralist Social Contract." *Yale French Studies*, no. 123 (2013): 145–165. https://www.jstor.org/stable/23645880.

Schneider, Pierre. "Paris: Fresh Look at Colette's Work." *The New York Times* (April 9, 1973). https://archive.nytimes.com/www.nytimes.com/books/99/10/17/specials/colette-fresh.html.

Schwartzbaum, Lisa. "The Best Movie about Israel and Gaza Came out 18 Years Ago." *The New York Times*, December 24, 2023. https://www.nytimes.com/2023/12/23/opinion/israel-gaza-munich.html.

Sedgwick, Eve Kosovsky. "Paranoid Reading and Reparative Reading; or You're So Paranoid you Probably Think This Introduction Is about You." In *Novel Gazing: Queer Readings in Fiction*. Edited by Eve Kosovsky Sedgwick, 1–37. Durham, NC: Duke University Press, 1997. https://read.dukeupress.edu/books/book/636/chapter/128566/Paranoid-Reading-and-ReparativeReading-or-You-re.

Seeger, Dan. "Œuvre: Minnelli: *Gigi*," *SpectrumCulture* (December 12, 2013). https://spectrumculture.com/2013/12/12/oeuvre-minnelli-gigi/.

Smith, Susan. "Singing Outside the Frame: The Female Voice-off in *Gigi* (Minnelli, 1958)." *CineAction*, no. 72 (spring 2007): 32+. https://archive.org/stream/CineAction.072/CineAction.072_djvu.txt.

Sollers, Philippe. *Portrait de femmes*. Paris: Gallimard, 2013.

Song, Sandra. "Denise Gough Defends Her Genderfluid Role as Missy in *Colette*." *Nylon*, September 20, 2018. https://www.nylon.com/articles/denise-gough-colette-interview.

Spanos, William V. "The Detective and the Boundary: Some Notes on the Postmodern Literary Imagination Autumn." *Boundary* 21, no. 1 (Autumn, 1972): 147–168.

Spillers, Hortense. "Mama's Baby, Papa's Maybe: An American Grammar Book." *Diacritics* 17, no. 2 (1987): 65–81. https://doi.org/10.2307/464747. Accessed Mar. 31, 2023.

———*Black, White, and in Color: Essays on American Literature and Culture*. Chicago: Chicago University Press, 2003.

Thurman, Judith. *Secrets of the Flesh*. New York: Alfred A. Knopf, 1999.

———Introduction to Gigi, *Julie de Carneilhan, Chance Acquaintances*. Translated by Roger Senhouse & Patrick Leigh Fermor, vii. New York: Farrar, Straus & Giroud, 2001.

———Review of the 2015 Broadway production of *Gigi*. "Good, Clean Fun: A Revival of '*Gigi*'." *New York Review of Books* (April 7, 2015). https://www.newyorker.com/culture/cultural-comment/good-clean-fun-a-revival-of-gigi.

———Introduction to *Chéri and the End of Chéri*. Translated by Paul Eprile, 7. New York: New York Review of Books Classics, 2022. Kindle.

Trésor de la langue française: Dictionnaire de la langue du XIXe et du XXe siècle (1789–1960). http://www.atilf.fr/tlfi.

Venuti, Lawrence. *The Translator's Invisibility: A History of Translation*. Oxford and New York: Routledge, 2008.

Watt, Ian. *The Rise of the Novel*. Oakland: University of California, 1957.

INDEX

Milton Keynes UK
Ingram Content Group UK Ltd.
UKHW031624061224
451881UK00002B/16

9 781839 990489